WHY I'M A JOURNALIST

Why be a journalist? It can be a difficult job with long hours, hard work and an uncertain future. Journalists face relentless criticism and an industry in transition. Aaron Chimbel has put together a collection of essays from working journalists who answer the question — why be a journalist? — with their personal stories of coming up, toiling in the field and writing important, career-defining stories. These journalists come from different platforms, beats and locations, offering varying accounts of the travails and rewards of being a working journalist across changing landscapes and timelines.

The essays in *Why I'm a Journalist* offer encouragement and wisdom about the path to being a reporter, a broadcaster, an editor or a media professional. This is a collection for students interested in the field, novices engaged with building their careers and seasoned pros looking to learn from their colleagues.

Aaron Chimbel is an associate professor of professional practice in journalism at Texas Christian University's Bob Schieffer College of Communication, where he has taught full-time since 2009.

WHY I'M A JOURNALIST

Personal stories from those who cover the news

Edited by Aaron Chimbel

Routledge
Taylor & Francis Group

NEW YORK AND LONDON

First published 2018
by Routledge
711 Third Avenue, New York, NY 10017

and by Routledge
2 Park Square, Milton Park, Abingdon, Oxon, OX14 4RN

Routledge is an imprint of the Taylor & Francis Group, an informa business

© 2018 Taylor & Francis

Library of Congress Cataloging-in-Publication Data
Names: Chimbel, Aaron, editor.
Title: Why I'm a journalist? : personal stories from those who cover the news / edited by Aaron Chimbel.
Description: New York : Routledge, 2017.
Identifiers: LCCN 2017004200| ISBN 9780415349215 (hardback) | ISBN 9780415349222 (pbk.) | ISBN 9781315229201 (ebk.)
Subjects: LCSH: Journalists—Biography.
Classification: LCC PN4820 .W59 2017 | DDC 070.922 [B]—dc23
LC record available at https://lccn.loc.gov/2017004200

ISBN: 9780415349215 (hbk)
ISBN: 9780415349222 (pbk)
ISBN: 9781315229201 (ebk)

Typeset in Bembo
by Apex CoVantage, LLC

*To the journalists around the world who have given their lives
in pursuit of the truth*

CONTENTS

Media journalists 49

Business journalists 67

Sports journalists 83

Print journalists 97

Broadcast journalists 111

Digital journalists 131

Journalism leaders 147

Young journalists 169

Afterword: My life in journalism 199

FOREWORD

Byron Pitts

"NIGHTLINE" CO-ANCHOR
ABC NEWS

Source: ABC News

Several times in my career I've been asked (mostly by college students and their parents) what was your "plan B"? In other words, if a career in journalism didn't work out what would you do for living? For my entire 34-year career I've only had one answer: "There was no plan B." All God gave me I'd give to this one profession.

I love journalism. Broadcast journalism in particular. It was the legendary Edward R. Murrow who said of TV news "it is merely wires and lights in a box" if not used properly. Too often in newsrooms across our great nation that's exactly what television journalism looks like: just wires and lights and pretty faces in a box. But at our best we are able to inform and enlighten and inspire like few mediums ever have.

Good journalism is a vital part of our glorious democracy. It's a solemn responsibility to shed light in dark places, to afflict the comfortable and comfort the afflicted and at the same time give voice to the voiceless. As someone who didn't learn to read until I was 12 years old and spoke with a stutter until my junior year in college, the task of giving voice to the voiceless is at the core of why I'm a journalist.

At this writing, journalistic credibility is at an all-time low. Many Americans don't trust the "mainstream" media, and perhaps for good reason. The optimist in me sees such ranking as a wonderful opportunity for those of us who work in the profession today and to those who will follow us. We must give the public good reason to trust us. If they don't, then we have failed the public and not the other way around. How do we regain their trust? It's pretty simple: accuracy, fairness, humility and hard work. My late mother believed "prayer and hard word could solve anything." And I learned years ago never to disagree with my mother.

More than a sacred responsibility, being a journalist (anywhere in the world) is a privilege. People invite us into their homes and businesses and private lives, often at when they are at their lowest and most vulnerable. They trust us to tell their truth with compassion and humility. At other times, we're asked to push back against powerful forces from governments to individuals who, maliciously or unintentionally, do harm to individuals or the masses. We, as journalists, get to hold those powerful forces accountable. And some days we get to cover history. On occasion we help to shape it. Unlike the many gifted people who chose medicine or science as careers, we rarely if ever save lives in journalism, but we can play a hand in making life better.

Pro tip

Read, read, read. Listen, listen, listen. Study great writing.

This wonderful profession has blessed me with the opportunity to cover three wars, interview the last six presidents of the United States and visit more than 40 countries. I've also witnessed two executions (the electric chair and lethal injection). It's allowed me to see human beings at their very best and their very worst. Each of those opportunities has left me convinced about the importance of journalism, which serves the dire need for accurate information that allows a democracy to function properly and provides the glimmer of hope journalism offers to people around the world in search of a better life and a more perfect union. Our world is flawed. Journalism most certainly is flawed. But through all that, journalism has taught me and allowed me to witness — it has left me deeply optimistic about the profession and our society. Journalism always needs new blood. The next generation more diverse, more talented than the generation that preceded it.

I've covered some of the darkest events in modern history (9/11, the wars in Iraq and Afghanistan, the earthquake in Haiti, the tsunami in Indonesia). In each place journalists helped the world make sense of each event — sometimes delivering the worst news imaginable (death tolls, detailing responsibility and casualty numbers), at other moments recounting moments of almost unimaginable joy or courage (people found alive in Haiti, the brave responders on 9/11).

And I've known colleagues who gave their full measure to our profession. Good and decent men and women. They were not "cowboys" or thrill seekers, rather they were men and women of conviction who had the courage to go into difficult situations in search of complicated truths.

Journalism isn't for everyone. If you're attracted to celebrity, go elsewhere. You want a cushy job or comfortable hours, don't bother to apply. There are a few people journalism has made rich, but all of us have certainly had our lives enriched. For me, next to my faith, my family and closest friends, journalism has meant everything to me. It's afforded me opportunities at the edge of my wildest dreams. It's challenged almost all of my preconceived notions, expanded my mind, toughened my hide and softened my heart and stripped bare my biases. I hope I've covered a story or two that in fact informed, enlightened and best of all inspired someone.

More than a fraternity, I've found journalism to be a calling of people who are at the very least curious, and many I've met along the way are deeply concerned about their community. And it doesn't matter the size of that community, from small town newspaper to covering the world. The core values of journalism remain the same: a commitment to truth, accuracy and fairness.

And so I am convinced when God calls me home, I can whisper to the angels: "My living has not been in vain" — in great part because I was blessed to be a journalist. Thus, there was never a need for a "plan B."

Bio

Byron Pitts was named ABC News "Nightline" co-anchor in 2014.

He joined ABC News in April 2013 as an anchor and chief national correspondent covering national news stories and in-depth features for the network, reporting for all broadcasts and platforms including "Good Morning America," "World News," "Nightline," "This Week" and "20/20." Pitts also reports for all ABC News digital properties including ABCNews.com.

Named the National Association of Black Journalists (NABJ) Journalist of the Year in 2002, Pitts is a multiple Emmy award-winning journalist known for his thoughtful storytelling, on-the-ground reporting and in-depth interviews.

A news veteran with more than 30 years of experience, Pitts has traveled around the world to cover some of the biggest news stories of our time from the Florida presidential recount to the tsunami in Indonesia and the refugee crisis in Kosovo. In less than 24 hours after joining ABC News, Pitts participated in live special coverage of the Boston marathon bombing investigation, including the day-long manhunt for the Tsarnaev brothers that virtually shut down the city.

Prior to joining ABC News, Pitts spent 15 years at CBS News, where he served as chief national correspondent for "CBS Evening News" and filed regularly for "60 Minutes," covering presidential campaigns and political conventions, the wars in Iraq and Afghanistan, Hurricane Katrina in New Orleans and the devastating earthquake in Haiti. He was also one of CBS News' first reporters at Ground Zero during the 9/11 terrorist attacks, winning an Emmy award for his coverage. Pitts has received several other prestigious awards for his work including an Emmy award for his reporting on the Chicago train wreck in 1999, a National Association of Black Journalists Award, four Associated Press Awards and six regional Emmy awards.

Byron joined CBS News in 1997 as a correspondent for the 24-hour affiliate news service, CBS Newspath, in Washington, D.C., where he focused on politics and national interest pieces. One year later, he was named CBS News correspondent, filing for the Miami and Atlanta bureaus before arriving in New York City in 2001.

Byron dreamed of becoming a journalist at a young age, but he faced two serious obstacles to his dream. He was illiterate until the age of 12 and struggled to overcome a stutter. Byron chronicled his journey in a 2009 memoir titled, "Step Out on Nothing: How Faith and Family Helped Me Conquer Life's Challenges."

He began his career at WNCT-TV in Greenville, North Carolina, where he covered local news and served as weekend sports anchor. He graduated from Ohio Wesleyan University in 1982, where he studied journalism and speech communication.

Byron Pitts is a native of Baltimore, Maryland, and he currently lives in New York City.

PREFACE

Aaron Chimbel

As a journalist, you have an important job, one that is the only profession mentioned by name in the U.S. Constitution as "the press" in the First Amendment.

In an interview on CBS' "Face the Nation" in 2013, the then-executive editor of the New York Times, Jill Abramson, issued a familiar refrain: "The First Amendment is first for a reason. Thomas Jefferson and James Madison thought it was crucial for our country to have a free and robust press to help keep the government accountable."

We journalists take our work seriously. The First Amendment is FIRST, damn it. Of course, never mind the history that the First Amendment was actually never intended to be the first among 10, but rather the third among 12 amendments in the Bill of Rights that Congress approved (the first two weren't approved by the states at the time).

Still, journalists rightly take their jobs seriously. You cannot have a free exchange of ideas and, thus, a democracy without a free press.

Journalists of all types and from many backgrounds share a singular focus. It's explained in the Society of Professional Journalists' Code of Ethics: Seek Truth and Report It.

For most journalists, the work is for the public good. It's work to provide a check on what those in power are doing. Journalism is often called the fourth branch of government or the Fourth Estate. It's often heady work that leads many people who want to make the world and their community better.

But, like many journalists, I also had a less than idealistic path to journalism. When I was in middle school, my mouth got the best of me on more than one occasion, and when it did my parents grounded me from watching television with one caveat: I could watch the news.

Thus, my obsession with journalism began. I remember watching the "Today Show" every morning when Bryant Gumbel and Katie Couric would take us around the world. It seemed like the best job in the world to question newsmakers and to go to the most fascinating places on earth.

Of course, I learned there's a lot more to journalism than just what I saw Bryant and Katie do on-air for a couple hours each day.

Reporting is hard work. Verifying information is time-consuming. Preparing stories for public consumption — and the scrutiny that comes with it — requires attention to detail and thoughtfulness.

It's often sitting around courthouses, or being battered by a hurricane. It's a lot of hurry up and wait. It's going to not very desirable places and to dangerous places. It's getting up really early and working non-stop. It's talking to people on their worst day.

But it's also telling the untold stories, being witness to history, questioning those in power, fostering discourse, leading to legislation being changed and, simply put, saving lives.

Journalists do and journalism does all of that — and more.

In this book, you'll hear from many journalists from a wide range of backgrounds who will tell you why they do this work. It can be glamorous, like being a network star as Bryant Gumbel and Katie Couric were when I first became hooked on journalism, but more realistically there is a lot of hard, tedious and unglamorous work that goes in to ensuring the best ideals of journalism and its place in democracy. Despite much criticism, these folks do this work for important reasons, even if how they got into it may have been for less than idealistic reasons.

Bio

Aaron Chimbel is an associate professor of professional practice in journalism at Texas Christian University's Bob Schieffer College of Communication, where he has taught full-time since 2009.

Chimbel teaches a variety of journalism classes and focuses on digital and broadcast news.

His academic writing has been featured in the Online Journalism Review, Convergence Newsletter, Newspaper Research Journal, The Journal of Social Media in Society, MediaShift, Electronic News, Journal of Media Education and College Media Review. He is also the author of "Introduction to Journalism," a textbook that corresponds with the TCU course of the same name he created.

Before TCU, Chimbel worked at WFAA-TV in Dallas-Fort Worth. He was hired as likely the first person at any local television station to produce original video content for the Web as the "MoJo" or mobile journalist for wfaa.com.

While at WFAA, Chimbel's work was honored numerous times by a variety of major organizations including the National Academy of Television Arts and Sciences, the Radio-TV News Directors Association, the National Press Photographers Association and the Texas Associated Press Broadcasters. He won five Advanced Media Emmys and was part of the WFAA team that was awarded a national Edward R. Murrow Award.

Before joining WFAA, Chimbel was a reporter for KWTX-TV and a producer at Texas Cable News. He has also produced two documentaries: "Soldier of God" chronicled the religious anti-war movement leading up to the 2003 war in Iraq and "Learning the Language" was an innovative web-based project examining Dallas' largest ESL-only program.

Chimbel graduated from TCU with a bachelor's degree in broadcast journalism. He also earned a master's degree from the Columbia University Graduate School of Journalism.

ACKNOWLEDGMENTS

I would like to thank several people who helped make this book a reality, starting with my wife, Bethanne, who is always so supportive of any project I undertake.

I am grateful to Ross Wagenhofer at Routledge/Taylor & Francis who saw the potential in this book and helped guide it to publication. In addition, his colleagues Nicole Salazar and Megan Hiatt have been invaluable resources for making this project a reality.

Most importantly, I would like to thank the dozens of journalists who gave their time and talents to help others understand why journalists do this important work. This book would not have been possible without their generosity.

Finally, I would like to thank my family for their endless love and support, including my dad, Joe, and my two amazing daughters, Claire and Dylan, who make every day joyful.

CONTRIBUTORS

Joel Anderson is a senior national writer at BuzzFeed News.

Alex Apple has worked as a reporter at WCAX-TV in Vermont and as a contributor at POLITICO and Professional Media Group.

Rose Baca is a staff photographer at The Dallas Morning News.

Peter Bhatia is the editor and vice president of the Cincinnati Enquirer.

Karen Blumenthal is an author and former Wall Street Journal reporter, bureau chief and columnist.

Ziva Branstetter is the editor-in-chief at The Frontier in Tulsa, Oklahoma.

David Cohn is a senior director at Alpha Group, Advance Digital.

Karen Crouse is a sportswriter covering golf at The New York Times.

Lexy Cruz is a news producer at KDFW-TV in Dallas.

Eric Deggans is the television critic for NPR.

Andrea Drusch is a congressional reporter at National Journal.

Can Dündar is the former editor-in-chief of the Cumhuriyet newspaper in Turkey.

Wayne Freedman is a reporter at KGO-TV San Francisco.

Lauren Galippo is an associate producer for "CBS This Morning."

Mark Godich is a senior editor at Sports Illustrated.

Kelli B. Grant is a personal finance and consumer reporter for CNBC.com.

Kristen Hare is a reporter for the Poynter Institute.

John F. Harris is the co-founder, publisher and editor-in-chief of POLITICO.

Tawnell D. Hobbs is national education reporter for The Wall Street Journal.

Carlos C. Hopkins is an executive producer at KNBC-TV/NBC Los Angeles.

Elise Hu is the Seoul bureau chief and an international correspondent for NPR.

Robyn Kriel is a correspondent and anchor for CNN.

Muhammad Lila is an international correspondent for CNN.

Aminda (Mindy) Marqués Gonzalez is the executive editor and vice president for news at the Miami Herald.

Andrea Masenda is an assistant editor at ESPN.

Michele Mitchell is an independent documentary filmmaker.

Steve Myers is the editor of The Lens in New Orleans.

Norah O'Donnell is a co-host of "CBS This Morning" and a contributor to "60 Minutes."

Ryan Osborne is a staff reporter for the Fort Worth Star-Telegram.

Byron Pitts is a co-anchor of "Nightline" at ABC News.

Lee Powell is a video reporter for The Washington Post.

Daniel Salazar is a county government reporter at the Wichita Eagle in Kansas.

Mila Sanina is the executive director and editor of PublicSource in Pittsburgh, Pennsylvania.

Bob Schieffer is the retired CBS News legend who was chief Washington correspondent and moderator of "Face the Nation."

Michael Schreiber is the founder of Amalgamated Unlimited.

Susana Schuler is the executive vice president of Raycom Media.

John Sharify is a contributing reporter at KING-TV in Seattle and the general manager of Seattle College's Cable Television and Seattle Community Media.

Jay Shaylor is the executive producer of CNN's "The Situation Room with Wolf Blitzer."

Brian Stelter is the senior media correspondent and host of "Reliable Sources" at CNN.

Perla Trevizo has covered the U.S.–Mexico border for the Arizona Daily Star.

Public affairs journalists

At its essence, journalism is about telling the public about what those in power are up to. The coverage of public affairs, politics and government is vital to democracy.

What do we really think those in positions of power would do if they were left free from journalistic coverage? How would citizens know what their representatives, from the school board to the U.S. Senate, are really up to?

However, the journalists who cover politics face intense scrutiny and their motives are often questioned. Politicians from Donald Trump to Bernie Sanders, Hillary Clinton to Ted Cruz and nearly everyone in between bemoan their perceived slights from or the biases of the journalists who cover them.

There is great distrust of mass media "to report the news fully, accurately and fairly," according to a Gallup study, which said trust in journalists reached a historic low in 2016. The study showed that just 32 percent of respondents say they "have a great deal or fair amount of trust in the media." When Gallup asked the same question in 1976, in the wake of the Watergate scandal, 72 percent of respondents trusted the media.

That context hangs over the work of journalists covering politics and public affairs, whose stories will be consumed by people interpreting them through their own biases.

No matter if they work for international news organizations like the Associated Press, local newspapers, legacy broadcasters or new digital ventures, these journalists face a constant barrage of spin, deception and distrust. It's a lot to deal with, yet these journalists rightly see their role as a crucial part of our democracy.

Work cited

Swift, A. (2016). Americans' Trust in Mass Media Sinks to New Low. Gallup. Retrieved from www.gallup.com/poll/195542/americans-trust-mass-media-sinks-new-low.aspx.

NORAH O'DONNELL

Co-host of "CBS This Morning" and contributor to "60 Minutes"

CBS News

Source: CBS News

I've still never been paid for the first article I wrote for a newspaper. Not a penny. And I don't care.

The thrill of seeing my byline on a Capitol Hill newspaper is something I'll never forget. I was 25 years old and had applied to work at Roll Call and pitched a piece on the rise of Rep. Patrick J. Kennedy, the nephew of Senator Ted Kennedy, who was then a rising star in the House of Representatives.

I spent three weeks reporting the piece that was published on October 23, 1997. The editor of the newspaper praised the piece and promised to call me back about a job offer. And then I never heard from her. Weeks passed, and I bombarded the receptionist about setting up a job interview with the editor, Susan Glasser.

Finally, a date was set. I arrived at the Roll Call offices and confidently introduced myself to the receptionist. "Oh, Ms. Glasser is not here today," she said. "But I have an appointment, a job interview," I replied. "I'm sorry. She's out sick, and I don't have any other information." I had woken up that morning convinced I was going to get a job, my first job as a newspaper reporter. Instead, I left on the verge of tears.

This story is now a lesson I give to lots of young women and men starting their careers. If you really want something, don't give up. And certainly don't believe that just because someone doesn't return your phone call or misses an appointment that it has anything to do with your ability or potential. Everybody is busy. I got that job several months later. And to this day, it's one of the best jobs I've ever had.

Beginning my career as a print journalist was probably the smartest career decisions I've ever made. Notebook and pen in hand, I could roam the august halls of Capitol Hill and interview congressmen and women! It was not only fun, but I also learned how to write, and I learned how to ask the right questions. Those skills got me noticed at age 25 by executives at NBC, CBS, ABC and CNN.

Pro tip

Show the people you interview respect, no matter their politics or their position.

I was hired as a network correspondent for NBC News just as cable news was burgeoning. That was critically important. Back then in the cutthroat atmosphere of broadcast news, you could spend days or weeks pitching a story and not get on the air. Fortunately, MSNBC needed to fill hours and hours of live programming. I was assigned to the White House and had to write a script every hour, sometimes 10 scripts a day! And let me add, there was no teleprompter. I memorized every single script or delivered them extemporaneously.

It was a crash course in live reporting. Even the graphic artists in the control room couldn't keep up. One time the producer didn't have time to finish the chyron under my name. Instead, it read, "Norah O'Donnell, The White Ho." Of course it should have labeled my location as, "The White House." At the time it was embarrassing. Now I think it's pretty funny.

My boss was Tim Russert, the Washington bureau chief for NBC News, and the longtime moderator of "Meet the Press." Every morning when I'd see him at the office, he'd say, "What do you know?" I think about that question every day. Tim helped me and trusted me. And to this day, I am grateful. He sent me around the world following Presidents Bill Clinton and George W. Bush. After the September 11 attacks, he assigned me to the Pentagon.

As a result, I can say I've been to every continent on the globe (except Antarctica) with either the president of the United States or the secretary of defense.

All those years on the road, traveling internationally, and crisscrossing the nation to cover five presidential campaigns, prepared me for my current position as co-host of "CBS This Morning."

I never dreamed of — or expected to — host a broadcast morning show. I was very happy in my role as chief White House correspondent for CBS News when they asked me to fill in for one week in July 2012. I had no expectations and figured it was a temporary assignment. Little did I know that Charlie Rose, Gayle King and I would click instantly. It was like we were old friends! By the third day, the legendary Bob Schieffer called me and said with his Texas twang, "Norah, I tell you what. They are gonna offer you that job! You are just too good." If you know Bob, you know he's about the most charming man alive. If you know Bob, you also know he's just about always right.

Days later, the top executives at CBS News called and asked if I would consider uprooting my whole family and moving from Washington to New York. It was not an easy decision, and to this day it is not easy living between two cities. But I got into journalism because I wanted a front row seat to history. I truly love the news. I wake up at 4:30 a.m. every day so excited to read five newspapers.

Plus, anchoring "CBS This Morning" is fun. To date, our show has the largest audience in CBS News history. I know we produce the very best broadcast every morning and there's one simple reason: the people that work on the show. No matter what you do, surround yourself with people who share your passion and work ethic. Just as important, find people you like and respect. Show the people you interview respect, no matter their politics or their position. Those simple things will get you very far in your career.

Bio

Norah O'Donnell is the co-host of "CBS This Morning." She also contributes to "60 Minutes" and fills in as anchor for the "CBS Evening News." O'Donnell joined "CBS This Morning" in July 2012. Prior to that, she served as CBS News chief White House correspondent.

Since joining "CBS This Morning," O'Donnell has interviewed President Barack Obama, Vice President Joe Biden for "60 Minutes," and some of the world's most notable figures, including His Royal Highness Prince Henry of Wales, Nobel Peace Prize winner Malala Yousafzai and the Dalai Lama. She won the Merriman Smith Memorial Award for excellence in presidential news coverage for her 60 Minutes interview with Vice President Biden and his wife, Dr. Jill Biden, on his decision not to run for president. O'Donnell also landed the first interview with NFL commissioner Roger Goodell at the height of the league's domestic violence scandal. She covered the historic election of Pope Francis in Vatican City as well as his first apostolic voyage to the United States. She also reported from the scenes of the San Bernardino terror attack and the Boston Marathon bombing, and was part of the CBS News team that received an Alfred I. DuPont Award for the network's coverage of the 2012 Newtown massacre.

O'Donnell was named "Broadcaster of the Year" by the New York State Broadcasters Association in 2014. Prior to joining CBS News, O'Donnell worked for more than a decade at NBC News, where she covered the Pentagon, Congress and the White House. Her assignments took her around the globe: she reported from every continent except Antarctica with either the president of the United States or the secretary of defense.

O'Donnell has covered a number of breaking news stories. She reported from the Pentagon on September 11, 2001, and received the prestigious Sigma Delta Chi Award for Breaking News Coverage for a "Dateline NBC" story titled "D.C. In Crisis." In the months following the attacks, she traveled extensively with then Secretary of Defense Donald Rumsfeld, including on his first trip to Afghanistan following the terrorist attacks.

O'Donnell was an NBC News White House correspondent during the 2004 presidential elections, covering the campaigns of then President George W. Bush and Senator John Kerry. Prior to covering the White House, O'Donnell was an NBC News congressional correspondent, reporting on the lead-up to the Iraq War. She also covered the 2000 presidential campaign. In all, O'Donnell has covered five presidential campaigns and reported from every political convention since then.

She began her career as a print reporter for Roll Call, a Capitol Hill newspaper, for which she covered the impeachment of President Clinton and traveled the country covering congressional elections.

A firm believer in empowering women, O'Donnell sits on the board of directors of the International Women's Media Foundation.

Born into a military family, O'Donnell grew up in San Antonio, Texas; Landstuhl, Germany; Seoul, South Korea; and Washington, D.C. She is a graduate of Georgetown University and received a Bachelor of Arts in philosophy as well as a Master of Arts in liberal studies. She is married to Geoff Tracy, a restaurateur in Washington, D.C. They have three children.

JOHN F. HARRIS

Co-founder, publisher and editor-in-chief

POLITICO

Source: Politico

Why would someone go into journalism?

For those of us in the POLITICO newsroom, this question, or its subsidiary — "Why should someone *stay* in journalism?" — is at the core of everything. As a practical matter, though, we hardly spend time with it. Editors are always answering why someone should come to POLITICO or, in this era of fierce competition for talent, why he or she should stay. That's different than the fundamental choice of why choose this career in the first place.

Beyond the newsroom, on our sales, technology, human resources and financial teams, slightly different versions of the same question echo: "What are we doing in the media business?" Perhaps friends and family put a sharper edge on it: "What the hell are you thinking?" Everyone knows the turmoil that has defined the news business for the past generation. Anyone smart enough to get hired at POLITICO knows that this disruption is likely to continue indefinitely, and has plenty of options in pursuits that may be more stable or more lucrative.

I'll answer what the hell I was thinking, some 30 years ago, and what I think now, which is the same in some ways but different in key respects. My conclusion is a mix of head and heart, but on any important decision these two should be aligned.

My head and heart both believe this: People who are exceptionally talented, disciplined and passionate about the media business can have more fun and more impact than ever before. And, with some good breaks, they can do better financially than ever before.

A warning: This optimistic appraisal applies for a relatively small stratum of people whose efforts (and maybe a measure of luck) manage to give them what economists call comparative advantage: something distinctive for which they are known in the marketplace. I'm rather dour, by contrast, on media for people who don't manage to attain one of those competitive levers. (I'm afraid my views are somewhat like those advertisements for prescription drugs, which open with smiling people free of heartburn or joint pain but then close with lengthy warnings about the risk of impotence or sudden death, and consult your doctor immediately if etcetera, etcetera).

Pro tip

Journalists should establish a franchise or area of expertise that they can do singularly well.

As I experienced it, I did not so much choose journalism as feel that it somehow chose me. I was in college, and a friend who was active on the student paper asked me to write a piece. I enjoyed it and wrote a couple more. Very suddenly, after never previously contemplating journalism, I decided this was what I was put on Earth to do. Without wishing to embrace mysticism, I felt as if some cosmic hand was pushing me to the right place, a sensation I have felt occasionally around other big choices in life, including the decision a decade ago to leave a comfortable professional home and start POLITICO.

Upon reflection, I think what appealed to me is that journalism is a composite that speaks to different sides of my temperament. In some moods, I am intrigued by people devoted to the "life of the mind," as on a college campus. But this choice would probably be frustrating to me over time — I like being near the action of large events. At the other end of the spectrum, I admire many people in public life, but I know well the sacrifices of personal freedom and compromises of conscience that are commonplace among people in politics. I've never had to do that in journalism.

I was captivated at age 18 by what still strikes me as the essential psychic lure of journalism — something that, in candor, first attracted me for self-gratifying rather than altruistic reasons. As a reporter, one has a license to overcome natural reticence or conventional courtesies and ask people questions, to follow personal curiosity where it takes you. Plus it was, and is, great fun to see your byline atop a piece, to take pleasure in a well-turned phrase, to have people react to what you write, in admiration or even in anger.

These pleasures, of course, are not (or at least should not be) by themselves sufficient to drive a career. My father was a surgeon, an idealistic man with a kind of dry, stoical style. He would always like to start conversations with his children by asking with a kind of playful half-smile, "So what did you do to make the world a better place today?"

Without wishing to sound like a Boy Scout, I regard the media business — whether working in the newsroom or supporting a publication in some other critical capacity — as a form of public service. In modest ways every day, and in large ways on big occasions, we are making the world a better place.

All these convictions, which first seized my thinking as a college freshman in the spring of 1982, still are the reasons why I'm a journalist. Journalism is a great career for someone who wants to do something worthwhile and get paid to have more fun at work than most people ever will. This is my response as to why a college freshman in 2016 would want to get into this profession. Or why younger journalists or media businesses or technology professionals, wisely asking themselves from time to time whether they are on the right long-term path, should stay on it.

But, but, but … there are some big things to think about. The incentives and opportunities of media, and the ways to climb the ladder, are different than they used to be.

When I was first attracted to this profession, we were living emphatically in an institutional age of journalism. A relatively small handful of media platforms had enormous power, largely unchallenged, to set the agenda of national affairs. What they decided was important — worthy of the front page or the evening news broadcast — is what everybody else in political and policy worlds treated as important. This editorial power was sustained by business models that made the institutions extraordinary amounts of money, and allowed them to cater to mass audiences with a general interest focus — coverage of Washington sitting side-by-side with foreign news, local news, movies and sports. Most of all, this era allowed editors to hire talented young people, train them as generalists, and inculcate them with a sense of institutional values and responsibilities.

The most important thing about you as a journalist was probably what came after your name. "Todd Purdum of The New York Times," to cite a colleague with whom I have often discussed these themes. Because of my interest in politics and national affairs, the institution that attracted me was The Washington Post.

Not long after becoming interested in journalism, I sat in the library one day devouring a long Q&A interview in American Heritage magazine with Ben Bradlee, the Post editor of Watergate fame, conducted by Des Moines Register editor Michael Gartner. Ben was talking, in his inimitable way (even though I used to do a pretty good Ben Bradlee imitation) about the power and mission of the Post. I re-read the interview a few months ago, when POLITICO won the Benjamin C. Bradlee Award from the National Press Foundation. You might find it interesting.

Within just a couple years, thanks to some lucky breaks (and I would say a kind of walk-through-glass determination) I found myself working at the Post, first as a summer intern and then a full-time reporter covering local news. I wonder if people now can appreciate how exciting it felt at age 21 to be in the midst (even if rarely in conversation), just across the newsroom, of figures who loomed so large in my imagination such as Bradlee, Mary McGrory, Bob Woodward or David Broder.

Were these and other journalists who cut such a wide path in those days larger figures than the ones in our midst now? Perhaps this is an optical illusion. As a young person who did not yet know these people well, I was aware of their achievements but not their infirmities, and not all the ways that reality can often fall short of legend.

In any event, I enjoyed the Post for two decades, and did well there. And then gradually — about a decade or so ago — it became plain to me that the institutional age of media was fading; just my luck as I was nearing the top of a now-troubled institution. In its place was emerging an entrepreneurial age of media.

What mattered in this age was not the legacy power of brands but the ability of individual journalists to have impact based on the power of their own expertise, creativity and authority.

POLITICO was born of this belief. We wanted to create a great institution but knew we were in an entrepreneurial age in which the fact that we were new, not anchored to old assumptions on either the editorial or business side, was a critical advantage.

And we knew the key to our success was establishing a roster of distinctive journalistic voices — a few established stars and a larger group whom we believed (and we were right in an impressive number of cases) would be future stars under our guidance.

My use of the phrase "stars" may sound facile, so I should qualify what I mean. An entrepreneurial age of media is also an individualistic age. This does not mean that it is important for everyone to get on TV or establish a flamboyant presence on social media. It does mean, in my mind, that the people with the most successful careers are those who establish a reputation within relevant communities for doing something singularly well — the comparative advantage that I mentioned earlier. Ambitious journalists, not necessarily at the very start of their career, but usually by the time they are a decade or so in, should establish what's sometimes called a "franchise."

John Bresnahan is not often on TV, but he is known as the best-sourced, toughest and most trustworthy reporter on Capitol Hill. That's his franchise. As an editor, Joanne Kenen knows more about health care policy than many of the health care policy officials she and her reporters cover. That's her franchise. Michael Kruse has a singular gift for illuminating character, and the infinitely absorbing ways in which people's past informs who they are in the present. That's his franchise, one that he has employed to wonderful effect for POLITICO readers over the past year in his highly original coverage of Donald Trump.

You'll never hear me say that institutional values don't matter at POLITICO. There are certain newspaper conventions and customs that I grew up with that are no longer relevant and can safely be discarded. But the task of contemporary editors is to defend and vindicate certain values — fairness, truth, relevance, brilliant storytelling, commitment to the public interest — that are timeless.

It's also true that in the old days institutions had a certain stolid benevolence that allowed people to be happily a bit aimless. You could be a solid citizen, a reliable generalist, maybe cover education for a while, then go abroad and come back and cover the environment, a little of this and a little of that, and have a very secure, very respectable career. No sensible person these days would regard this kind of path as a sound strategy for career success.

Journalism will always welcome generalists. And I would say journalism, and other lines of the media business, will always be a great adventure for talented people in their 20s and 30s. You get to meet interesting people, hop on the occasional airplane, have interesting stories to share in the conversation at parties. Along the way, you learn a wealth of knowledge about the way the world runs that is valuable even if you eventually wind up in a different line of work.

But I observe that the media professionals who are building careers that carry them through a professional lifetime, who are reaping the greatest psychic rewards and the greatest financial ones, are organizing their efforts around making themselves the very best at some important facet of the craft.

I believe POLITICO has a comparative advantage of its own in this environment, since we're a highly focused publication, dedicated to dominating the politics and policy space, rather than a general interest platform organized around chasing every latest thing.

No matter how much disruption and reinvention the business goes through, and no matter how much heartache befalls legacy publications that don't adapt or new media experiments that don't work out, journalists, technologists and business professionals who make themselves singularly good at something important will always do very well.

Those are the people who can give the most convincing, and most exuberantly optimistic answer to the question, "Why would someone go into journalism?"

As for my own choices, I think of the answer Ben Bradlee gave in that American Heritage interview. Asked by Gartner if he would do it all again, Bradlee answered, "I would do it so fast! I wonder what took me so long, till I was sixteen, when I got my first job as a copy boy."

Bio

John F. Harris stumbled into journalism during his freshman year at Carleton College in Minnesota. His friend worked for the student newspaper and asked him to write a couple of articles. He did, and the effect was instantaneous. Suddenly, he was certain what he wanted to do in life.

Harris had always been fascinated by Washington and politics, and immediately had his sights on The Washington Post. Thanks to some good luck, he got there sooner than he could have reasonably expected, graduating from college on a Saturday in June 1985 and starting as a summer intern on the Monday. At the end of the summer, editors asked him to hang around a while longer.

That ended up being more than 21 years. At the Post, Harris covered local politics, state politics in Virginia and national politics. From 1995 to 2001, he covered the Clinton White House. Later, he expanded on that reporting in a history of Bill Clinton's presidency, "The Survivor: Bill Clinton in the White House." Harris is also co-author, with Mark Halperin, of a book on presidential politics, "The Way to Win: Taking the White House in 2008."

After 20 years as a reporter, Harris became drawn to editing. In part, this was just a sense that he had been around the track plenty of times and was ready for something different. Even more, however, it was a conviction that, at a time when journalism is undergoing wrenching upheavals, everyone who cares about the profession should be involved in answering the question, "What's next?" Becoming an editor was a way to be more immersed in those conversations about the future — about how to use the web more creatively, about how to sustain serious journalism at a time of diverse threats.

His brief editing career led him and Jim VandeHei — a colleague at the Post and partner at The Politico — to have blue-sky conversations about what they would do if they ever had the chance to start a publication about politics from the ground up. Those conversations were mostly a way of passing the time. Then, in the fall of 2006, they became a lot more serious. Robert Allbritton made clear that his notions about the future of journalism were very much in sympathy with theirs. He offered Harris and VandeHei the chance to start something from scratch, and they took it.

That is how they wound up at The Politico (the print newspaper in Washington) and Politico.com (the way their work will reach a much larger audience around the country). They have assembled a team of reporters and editors who will wake up each day looking for fresh ways to attack the best political stories in and around Capitol Hill and on the 2008 campaign trail.

Along the way, they hope to add to the conversation about what's next for journalism. And they are determined to have fun while doing it — something that is in lamentably short supply in newsrooms these days.

Putting out a new publication is hard work — and would be impossible if not for the people helping Harris on the home front. He is married to Ann O'Hanlon, and they live with their three children — Liza, Griffin and Nikki — in Alexandria, Va.

PERLA TREVIZO

Border reporter

Arizona Daily Star

Twelve years into my career, I increasingly find myself having to defend "the media." Whether we are corrupt. Whether we are doing our jobs. Whether we serve special interests — the list goes on and on.

For me, the comments are directly related to immigration and refugees, the issues I focus on and the people who continue to be a source of fear and easy scapegoating for many throughout the world. Some argue that we only cover positive stories, ignoring legitimate concerns from residents. For others, we only write about crime and negative aspects about immigration, ignoring all the good that comes with it.

When I became a journalist it never crossed my mind that part of my job would be to defend the profession I chose to practice. While there is a lot of room for improvement and reflection on how we do our job, including racial and cultural diversity inside newsrooms, the monolithic media that is the target of derision does not exist and we as journalists should not be intimidated.

As our society continues to fracture, as division fosters the worst in us, what we do is more important than ever. We have to be responsible, learn about and understand what we cover and always remember to honor those who are allowing us to share their stories.

I am proud to be a journalist who is able to give a voice to those who don't have one. And while I didn't start out wanting to go into journalism, looking back I realize I had a calling.

As a young child, I was more into jobs that got to wear cool uniforms, maybe a nurse or a flight attendant, I thought. Never mind that my grade school report on pandas was a thoroughly reported exposé on how cute they were or that my relatives always thought of me as the kid with all the questions, the one who always wanted to know the whys and hows.

In high school, a government class turned me on to politics and I was sure I wanted to be a lawyer. In college, my major was political science but I spent two semesters abroad, in Italy and Spain, learning more about the people and culture than whatever requisite-fulfilling class I was taking. Still, my course was set, so I applied to law school even if I couldn't convincingly put into words why I should be there, or how being an attorney would mesh with my desire to help people, to explore the world and to learn.

I was lucky that my lack of imagination helped the admissions department see through me. I was even luckier when a friend recommended me to a Spanish-language newspaper that was looking to expand. Why they hired me, I'll never know. I had not written professionally in Spanish and my first stories had more thesis statements than nut graphs, but I immediately fell in love with journalism, and with the help of my wonderful, patient colleagues I quickly grew as a young reporter.

There have certainly been ups and downs as the print industry struggles to reinvent itself. But there have always been those who believed in my work and have opened doors that led to more opportunities.

Pro tip

Never make the story about you, always respect the people you are writing about, and remember why you do the work you do. Don't be afraid to collaborate with reporters from other media outlets, it will make the story stronger and increase your reach.

Early in my career I accepted a position as a diversity reporter in Tennessee. It was my first time visiting the South and I remember being on a small plane from Dallas on my way to the interview in Chattanooga. I was the only Hispanic on board. I had never paid much attention to ethnicity or immigration. Being from El Paso, Texas, where about 80 percent of the population looked and talked like me, I had not given it a second thought. But as I arrived and took a position at this new place, I better understood what it meant to be a minority.

My job, and my personal goal, was to introduce readers to the newcomers they were seeing around their neighborhoods and the new languages they were

hearing at the supermarket — changes that in some small towns had led to ordinances that limited how many people live in a single house, how many cars can be parked outside a home, or state bills requiring English to be the official language. I wanted to give people what they needed to make an informed decision. I never intended to tell readers what to do, but simply show who this "other" was.

I also had to gain the trust of these newcomers, to learn about them so they would allow me to tell their stories, their successes and their challenges. Being there for the day-to-day stories gave me access when a raid by immigration officials at the chicken processing plant became national news. It gave me the chance

to follow the families who returned to their native Guatemala and the immigration process that followed for those who stayed.

Learning more about Islam and the Muslim community to tell stories of day-to-day life, not just the obligatory community reaction to the latest headlines, was also rewarding but challenging. Many were suspicious of the media and wary about my intentions. Yet years after leaving Tennessee, when the city and the Muslim community were thrust into those headlines after a mass shooting, I received a Facebook message that read: "I know you are not in Chattanooga anymore but we in the Islamic Center miss you a lot. Pray for us and our city."

As gratifying as being remembered was, not all interactions are as positive. Being an immigrant and Hispanic covering diversity and immigration issues — in both Tennessee and Arizona — has also meant personal insults, questions about my legal status and my right to be in the United States. A reader once sent an anonymous handwritten letter telling me to go back "to wherever I came from" and demanded I take the blacks with me.

Not too long ago, a reader calling himself Big Ray wrote: "Maybe we should electrify the fence to keep the little greasy bastards out. You must be a wetback yourself I hope they break there [sic] fucking necks. Have a nice day."

Fortunately, such extremely negative reactions are in the minority. Sometimes an angry phone call or nasty email will end with a civil discussion. When you take time to listen and to respond, readers appreciate having someone take their concerns seriously.

There is nothing I would rather be than a journalist, so I am thankful I get to be one every day. I have been able to tell stories large and small, been read by many and by few, recognized with awards and summarily ignored. Whichever way it goes, as long as you're doing what you love, it's all worth it.

I was given the opportunity to go into this profession without any prior experience, without any clips under my belt and zero awards. With less and less positions out there and the many ambitious and prepared students coming out of journalism school, I don't think I would be so fortunate today. But maybe that's a good thing. It means we have many young people entering the profession more prepared than ever, ready to start making a difference from day one.

While the fate of the industry remains in flux, now is not the time to avoid going into journalism because the future is uncertain. On the contrary, it's an opportunity to work together to shape a new future.

Bio

Born in Ciudad Juárez, Mexico, and raised across the border in El Paso, Texas, Perla Trevizo has covered immigration stories for more than a decade from eight countries across America, Africa and Europe. She has received national and state awards for her coverage on immigration including the Dori J. Maynard Award for Diversity in Journalism, the National Edward R. Murrow Award for news documentary and the French-American Foundation's Immigration Journalism Award. She obtained a bachelor's in political science from the University of Texas at Austin and a master's in news agency journalism from the Universidad Rey Juan Carlos in Spain.

Career timeline

2016–present, Robert Bosch Foundation Fellowship in Germany.

2012–2016, border reporter at the Arizona Daily Star in Tucson.

2007–2012, covered immigration and diversity issues for the Chattanooga-Times Free Press in Tennessee.

2007, reporter at the El Paso Times.

2006, completed a master's in news agency journalism in Madrid and interned for the news agencies Efe and Dow Jones.

2005, reporter and editor weekly publications, the English-language Eastside Reporter and the Spanish-language El Paso y Más, as well as some reporting for the El Paso Times.

2004–2005, among a small team of journalists who launched El Diario de El Paso, a Spanish-language daily newspaper.

ZIVA BRANSTETTER

Editor-in-chief

The Frontier
Tulsa, Oklahoma

I was nine years old when President Richard Nixon — looking pale and shaken — told the nation he was resigning.

Seated on my living room floor on the evening of August 8, 1974, I had a notebook ready and a pen in hand as I watched Nixon speak on our tiny black-and-white TV set. I knew I was witnessing history and that meant I should record it.

I can trace my decision to become a journalist to moments like that one, where I realized the power of investigative journalism to expose corruption at the highest level.

Raised by a single father — a physics professor active in many political causes — I was imbued with the notion that few things were more important than making a difference in the world. My father also constantly reminded me that few things were worse than being a quitter. If there's one quality I am known for as a journalist, it's my tenacity.

I wasn't a particularly good student in high school but one subject held my interest: writing.

Filling out college applications, I came to the part where students are asked to declare a major. I didn't hesitate in choosing journalism; no other career even came to mind.

During the next four years at Oklahoma State University, I felt the thrill of a scoop but also the angst of difficult editorial decisions. I had to refuse a friend's request to omit her arrest from our published list of campus crimes.

I landed an internship at a feisty afternoon paper, The Tulsa Tribune. It was at "the Trib" — an editor-driven paper of the first order — that I first encountered actual investigative journalists. I was smitten with the place. These people were fearless and refused to accept anything less than the best from the staff.

Luckily, I wound up back at the Tribune after college as a rookie reporter. The editors pushed me and other reporters hard and, in turn, we pushed the people we covered hard, for information, records and answers. I knew better than to return to the newsroom with holes in a story.

The Trib's investigative team was led by one of the premier journalists in the nation, Mary Hargrove. Her reporting on the failure of an Oklahoma bank won a slew of awards, national attention and a term as board president of Investigative Reporters and Editors Inc. (IRE). (I would later go on to become vice president of IRE's board.)

While I was too inexperienced to work on Mary's team back then, observing the meticulous way the team approached investigative projects left a lasting impression.

One of my earliest forays into investigative reporting came when a young woman called me to say she'd been beaten by a jailer after her arrest in a nearby town. After reviewing medical records and photos of her injuries, I dug into the officer's background and found he'd been fired for using excessive force on prisoners at another jail. My stories prompted the department to fire the officer and also fueled my desire to take on more complex stories.

In 1990, I covered the first of four executions I've witnessed, a lesson in the importance of maintaining a professional demeanor while covering a difficult story. The experience served me well after Timothy McVeigh blew up the Oklahoma City federal building, killing 168 people, and after a tornado plowed through Joplin, Mo., killing 158.

The Tribune went the way of the rest of America's PM newspapers when it folded in 1992. I mourned the loss of that job deeply but treasure the lessons I learned there. Although I landed a good job in the Philadelphia Daily News' features section, I yearned to be back in news, telling stories that could dramatically impact people's lives.

I returned to Tulsa as a beat reporter for the morning newspaper, the Tulsa World, eventually working my way into an enterprise reporting job. I realized around this time that opportunities for accountability journalism were literally everywhere. You just needed the right tools, which increasingly meant you needed to understand how to obtain and analyze data.

After a week of IRE boot camp to learn these new skills, I was armed with a new ability to unlock secrets buried in seemingly boring government records.

Pro tip

Be hungry and hustle. I've known a lot of lucky reporters. I don't know any lazy lucky reporters. Develop sources and take care of them. Learn how to use Excel and always do a chronology of events with complex stories. It helps you see patterns.

A database of death certificates spanning a decade revealed more than 1,000 people had died in Oklahoma nursing homes from preventable causes such as falls and strangulation on bed rails. A database kept by the state's environmental agency revealed the names of Oklahoma's worst polluters and the fact that the state wasn't doing much to punish them.

I also discovered what to do when there is no database: create one. I built a database from paper records kept by an obscure but important state agency that licensed nursing home administrators. The results showed a clear pattern of foot dragging by the board members, most with deep ties to the nursing home industry, followed by decisions in nearly every case to dismiss the complaints.

The series of stories had the most dramatic results to that point in my career when the governor dismissed the entire board and formed a new one. Citizens can look up the complaint history of any nursing home administrator on the state's website as a result of those stories.

The importance of sources also became apparent. I'd always maintained ties with a few people who called to tip me off about stories. As the stories I wrote began to have more impact, my source list grew. Some of my ties with sources go back more than 20 years. One of them told me to check out the state lawmaker who owned rental properties so dilapidated that the city of Tulsa was threatening to tear them down. That led to a story about the lawmaker threatening city employees that he would write legislation removing the city's authority to tear down blighted properties.

Luckily, the code enforcement department taped all of its phone calls so when the lawmaker denied making such a threat, I was able to produce proof that he was lying. The lawmaker ended up losing his bid for re-election and being charged with a crime due to our continued reporting on his real estate business.

Another investigation I produced exposed rampant waste of public funds by the local ambulance authority, a government agency. The agency's director flew first class to conferences using a doctor's note saying he needed more seat space due to health issues. Lavish retirement parties featured gifts worth hundreds of dollars and the agency had a cozy relationship with its main contractor that resulted in numerous conflicts of interest.

A state audit backed up my findings and the agency overhauled its financial practices, putting rules in place to limit such excess in the future.

Through two decades at the Tulsa World, I was fortunate to have many opportunities like this to expose hypocrisy, corruption and wrongdoing and to write stories that helped the powerless.

As an editor, I helped one of my reporters investigate the case of Sheila Devereux, a woman sentenced to life in prison for a relatively minor drug crime due to Oklahoma's "three strikes you're out" law. In her file, we found names of several officers convicted of corruption in an unrelated case.

As a result of our stories, prosecutors agreed to a deal that allowed Sheila to be released and she remains free today, working, paying taxes and enjoying her grandchildren. One of the reasons I've stayed in Tulsa is that it's a small enough town to see the impact of stories like this.

The most important stories of my career so far occurred during the past several years. In 2014, I witnessed a fourth execution and this time things went terribly wrong. The inmate, Clayton Lockett, writhed in pain and mumbled for several minutes before the execution was halted and the blinds were closed. He died 43 minutes later.

My reporting partner, Cary Aspinwall, and I spent months investigating Oklahoma's deeply flawed death penalty process. Our stories showed that the state's obsession with keeping the process secret was largely to blame for the botched execution, which gave the state an international black eye.

Reporting on this subject in Oklahoma, where the death penalty enjoys wide support, brought a higher level of public scrutiny and criticism than I had experienced in the past. Some critics said the stories Cary and I wrote showed sympathy for Lockett, a convicted murderer. We understood the criticism even if we didn't agree with it, and that's why our series started off with a lengthy narrative focused on Lockett's victim.

At one point, we were told to stop using the word "botched" to describe the execution and the attorney general visited our publisher to complain about our reporting on the subject.

Along with the World, I sued Gov. Mary Fallin over her office's refusal to release emails about the execution. It was the first of several open records lawsuits I have filed against public officials.

Cary and I were thrilled and honored to be named finalists in the local reporting category of the Pulitzer Prizes for our reporting on the execution.

In 2015, I teamed up with another reporter, Dylan Goforth, to investigate the Tulsa County Sheriff's Office after a volunteer reserve deputy fatally shot an unarmed man.

Reserve Deputy Robert Bates was a wealthy friend of the longtime sheriff, who had ignored many warnings that his 73-year-old fishing buddy was completely unqualified for the job. Our investigation unearthed a report detailing how Sheriff Stanley Glanz and his top advisors had covered for Bates and even ordered employees to falsify training records.

The top officials in the sheriff's office resigned one by one. Glanz was charged with two misdemeanor counts and resigned in disgrace and Bates was convicted of manslaughter in the shooting, which he said was an accident.

I've since left the World to start The Frontier, a website focused on local investigative and enterprise reporting, along with three other reporters who worked with me at the newspaper. The former publisher of the Tulsa World, Robert Lorton III, founded our site.

I'm continuing to do the kind of watchdog work for The Frontier that I did at the newspaper but am enjoying experimenting with new ways to tell stories. I'm no longer concerned about public officials or advertisers pressuring my bosses due to my reporting. As a nonprofit, we have no advertisers. My bosses are the readers.

As I look back on my career, which has now spanned nearly three decades, I can see a thread running through all of my stories. It was my father's advice: Go make a difference in the world and never quit.

Bio

Ziva Branstetter is editor-in-chief of The Frontier, a website devoted to investigative and enterprise news in Oklahoma. She previously spent more than 20 years as an editor and reporter at the Tulsa World, most recently as the enterprise editor.

In 2015, Branstetter and her reporting partner, Cary Aspinwall, were finalists for the Pulitzer Prize in local reporting, the Anthony Shadid Ethics in Journalism Award and the Scripps Howard Service to the First Amendment Award. They have won numerous other national and state awards for their reporting.

Previously, Branstetter worked for The Tulsa Tribune and the Philadelphia Daily News.

Branstetter is vice president of the board of Investigative Reporters and Editors Inc. She has also served as president and board member of Freedom of Information Oklahoma Inc., a nonprofit watchdog group devoted to open government. She is a graduate of Oklahoma State University.

Career timeline

2015–present, editor-in-chief, The Frontier in Tulsa, Oklahoma.

1994–2015, state reporter, city hall reporter, assistant city editor, city editor and enterprise editor at the Tulsa World.

1992–1994, assistant editor and writer, features section of the Philadelphia Daily News.

1988–1992, police reporter, state reporter and assistant city editor at The Tulsa Tribune.

International journalists

The glamor of traveling the world to cover stories of global importance makes being an international correspondent seem like something out of a movie.

Then there is the reality. Covering hot spots is dangerous, tiring and far from leisurely enjoying the cafés of Paris.

The Committee to Protect Journalists reports that more than 1,200 journalists have been killed covering news or because of their work around the world since 1992. Many more have been imprisoned or exiled for their efforts to bring information to the public.

Americans often take for granted the press freedoms guaranteed by the First Amendment, but a free press is, in fact, a foreign concept for most people in the world. Just 13 percent of people live in a country with a free press according to Freedom House, an independent organization that tracks press freedom around the world, which notes that press freedoms have declined in recent years.

For journalists, this means working in a precarious situation. The government may not want you to do your work and terrorist groups or drug lords may try to kill you. Journalists are in the firing line when covering conflicts and wars.

Despite all this, men and women from around the world — including many from news organizations based in the United States — put themselves in danger because the truths of what is going on are that important.

The best way to understand what is really going on in Syria or North Korea or Haiti is to go there and bear witness. The rest of the world is counting on it.

Works cited

Committee to Protect Journalists (2016). Retrieved from www.cpj.org.
Freedom House (2016). Freedom of the Press 2016. Retrieved from https://freedomhouse. org/report/freedom-press/freedom-press-2016.

ELISE HU

International correspondent and Seoul bureau chief

NPR

People sometimes talk about how love isn't a choice. They had lists of certain traits they wanted from a life partner but then when they met the right mate, none of it mattered. In much the same way, I don't think becoming a journalist was much of a choice for me. I knew from when I was eight years old that news reporting is what I was going to do. By seventh grade, I had decided on a beat. I found a typed paper from Mrs. Blackmore's language arts class a few years back, when cleaning out my stuff from childhood home. Here's what it read (pardon the seventh-grade level writing):

I found what I wanted. It was the aspiration to become a political news journalist. Let's examine the facts.

a)   I love politics. I find it interesting and feel it is a field that takes a lot of work and critical thinking. I also like it because of the involvement of the people in the field.

b)   I love news and current events.

c)   I like to write about the news. Actually, I like to write about any interesting topic, and the news is constantly changing so I think it would be very interesting to write about.

None of those things have fundamentally changed. Today I cover geopolitics, which I guess you can call political news on a global scale. And I get to do it from a country that was foreign to me even as a tourist: South Korea. And I do it because in a lot of ways I know nothing else. This was less of a conscious choice than something I knew from when I was four feet tall that I would do.

As an adult, I also know what I don't want. I don't want a desk job. I don't want a routine. I don't want a sense that I go to work every day at the same place.

My work places, instead, are strangers' living rooms and mansions and trailer parks. They are border villages where sweet potatoes are cooked over a coal-fired heater in the middle of a primitive convenience store. (I should have put convenience store in quotes; there was nothing really convenient about it.) I work in museums dedicated to ramen noodles. And in Ford Explorers parked too close to fast-swelling rivers following a hurricane. And huddled on risers cramped with too many cameras on election night.

There is so much to discover and try to understand about the world and communities and people dissimilar from us. Being a news reporter is a window to all of that, with the added benefit of getting paid along the way. I am a witness to some serious degeneracy (I covered a man-on-dog rape one time, no joke), but also some moments of unbridled love and humanity. I get to interview innovators and artists and certified geniuses and learn a little bit of something from all of them. It's an endless, every day education.

It is as a journalist that I've gotten to explore 40 countries and counting. Seeing so much and meeting so many people and witnessing such a range of culture is rather life-altering, not to be too hyperbolic about it. Do you want to challenge your assumptions? Be a journalist. Do you want to shift your perspective? Be a journalist. Do you want to widen your understanding of the places and spaces we move in? Be a journalist. There is no better career for a curious person who never wants to stop learning and growing.

Our highest calling to achieve — at least as journalism has been practiced in the West post-Watergate — is to affect change, challenge institutions of power and expose wrongdoing in the public interest. I think that's incredible and noble, but that needn't be the key reason to do what we do, because honestly, so much of my career at the start was covering Saturday job fairs in junior high gymnasiums or standing in the pitch black, outside school board meetings at 10 p.m. for a live shot, hours after the meeting had concluded. And yet I still got something out of it, even though sometimes I'd say out loud, "I got a college degree for this?" Now that I'm older I realize it prepared me for what I do now, which is more along the lines of riding in speeding motorcades with the U.S. Treasury secretary as we zoom down giant Beijing thoroughfares that have been closed down for his arrival.

Pro tip

Find a mentor or mentors that you trust and can build a relationship with over time. They will help you throughout your career, as you make difficult decisions or just face insecurities about your day-to-day work. Mentors are also linked into networks and you never know who in their orbit might be able to change your life later on.

Which is to say, this is also the kind of work in which you can keep getting better — and the gig keeps getting better — with more experience. I know how to listen better now. And to ask certain questions that I wouldn't have earlier in my career. Or to just wait someone out after a surface-level answer, in the hopes of getting something more real, more human. Because beyond the watchdogging type of journalism is more common, but just as valuable, kind: showing or educating our audiences, adding context to help them better understand our spaces and places. We can help answer questions our community members have. We can, in our storytelling, help foster better understanding between ideas or people that may not otherwise have known about one another.

I see that as more important to my work as a foreign correspondent than trying to be a scoop machine. Asia, in particular, is seen as "exotic" and "foreign" and part of it is because the culture is so different from the West, and part of it is that there's so much to learn about the world and world history in school that Asia often comes in the May and June months when school is about to be over. Maya Angelou famously said we're all more alike than we are unalike; and in that way my role in Asia is partially diplomatic — acting as a bridge between two cultures, helping interpret the East to the West, fostering a better understanding, making plain the obvious similarities, interrogating the differences, adding layers to what can otherwise be way oversimplified takes on a dynamic and growing continent where half of all humanity lives.

Now I have to get to the part about money. I don't make a lot of it, comparatively speaking. That's kind of a given in journalism, and especially in public media, in which I toil. This is also an industry that has shed tens of thousands of jobs in the years since I graduated from college. I have thrown and attended too many goodbye parties for departing colleagues. Colleagues who are more talented than me by a magnitude of a thousand. So it goes without saying that it is against the odds and rather improbable that I am still a journalist today, given the bad business prospects of the industry at large.

But I also think experience and understanding is invaluable, and that's what my life in journalism has paid me, in spades. What I've witnessed and shared with the world gives me purpose and meaning. And while I do not wish upon you, future journalists, the experience of spending the night in an airport baggage claim without heat or covers, or the close calls of your news vehicle being engulfed in flooding waters, they do make for awesome stories. And it's a huge privilege to collect them still, decades after my eight-year-old self knew I'd report for a living.

Bio

Elise Hu is an international correspondent for NPR, an American radio and digital news network that reaches 26 million weekly listeners. She is the founding Seoul, South Korea bureau chief for the network and her reporting takes her to several countries across East Asia.

She joined NPR in 2011 to coordinate the digital launch of StateImpact, a multi-station effort to improve coverage of state governments in local communities.

Before that, Hu was a founding journalist at The Texas Tribune, a digital news startup based in Austin, Texas, which focuses on investigative and explanatory reporting of state government. There, she reported stories for television and newspaper partners such as The New York Times but spent most of her time leading multimedia and social media reporting efforts, launching and hosting the weekly Texas Tribune 'Tribcast' and pioneering new forms of video storytelling on the web.

Hu's reporting work has earned a Gannett Foundation Award for Innovation in Watchdog Journalism, a National Edward R. Murrow Award for best online video, beat reporting awards from the Texas Associated Press and The Austin Chronicle once dubiously named her the "Best TV Reporter Who Can Write."

Outside of work, Hu has taught digital journalism at Northwestern University and Georgetown University's journalism schools and previously served as a guest co-host for TWIT.tv's program, "Tech News Today." She's currently guest co-hosting "Foreign Correspondents," a weekly program on Korea's English language network, Arirang. She's also an adviser to the John S. and James L. Knight Foundation, where she gets the cool job of keeping up with emerging media and technology as a panelist for the Knight News Challenge.

A television news reporter for the first part of her career, Hu previously worked as the state political correspondent for KVUE-TV in Texas and WYFF-TV in South Carolina. She started her post-college career at KWTX-TV in Waco, Texas, where during coverage of President George W. Bush's "Western" White House, she got to go out on her first dates with her now-husband, who is also a journalist.

Hu graduated magna cum laude from the University of Missouri-Columbia's School of Journalism, a place she briefly left to study Mandarin Chinese in Taipei, Taiwan. While there, she contributed business and features reporting to The Taipei Times, an English-language daily. Her first job in journalism was as a teenage intern and production assistant for WFAA-TV in Dallas, Texas, her hometown.

She lives in Seoul with her husband, two human daughters and two cat sons.

Career timeline

2015–present, international correspondent and Seoul, South Korea bureau chief for NPR.

2013–present, technology and culture reporter for NPR.

2011–2013, digital editorial coordinator at NPR.

2009–2011, political reporter/multimedia projects at The Texas Tribune.

2006–2009, political reporter at KVUE-TV in Austin, Texas.

2004–2006, reporter at WYFF-TV in Spartanburg, South Carolina.

2003–2004, reporter and producer at KWTX-TV in Waco, Texas.

MUHAMMAD LILA

International correspondent

CNN

Some people have really cool stories about why they became journalists. It might involve a vacation overseas as a child, a class field trip to a newsroom or even delivering newspapers as a kid.

Mine starts with milk and wafers.

I grew up on an ordinary street in the suburbs of Toronto. Every night, my father had a ritual. At 10 p.m., he would come downstairs to watch the news. This was way before Twitter, Facebook, Insta — you name it. In those days, the only way to see what was happening in the world was to watch TV, and Canada's top national newscast aired at 10 p.m. I have vivid memories of watching those newscasts, my father eating grapes and me having my milk and wafers.

I'm not sure which I enjoyed more, hearing all the strange-sounding names of people and places around the world, or the wafers. Either way, I was hooked. I remember showing up to elementary school excited about what I'd seen the night before. While kids were talking about their favorite cartoons or baseball players, I wanted to talk about how Imelda Marcos had a huge shoe collection, or how Saddam had used chemical weapons against the Kurds. When my childish excitement was met with blank stares of disapproval, it only convinced me even more. Growing up, I knew that the world was full of incredible and amazing stories — of people whose names I couldn't pronounce, countries where pirates still existed and rainforests where mysterious tribes have never seen the outside world.

At the time, I didn't think I'd be the one to tell those stories. But I knew I wanted to be there — on the ground — as those stories were happening.

Somewhere along the line, I wound up realizing that I was a natural storyteller. I remember in Mr. Yeoh's seventh-grade science class when he gave us a home-work assignment to label the different parts of an amoeba. To this day, I couldn't tell you why on earth anyone needs to know the different parts of an amoeba (I mean, seriously!). Instead of doing the assignment, I broke the rules, and wrote a short story instead. The following week, Mr. Yeoh gathered everyone around the table and announced that only one person hadn't done the assignment. He made me read the story out loud, in front of the class. It felt like a punishment. The story was about a friend of mine who developed superpowers and used them to help solve the world's garbage crisis. I kind of wrote it on a whim, mostly because I was bored, but also because I didn't really care much for amoebas. After I read the story loud, I was so embarrassed. I thought Mr. Yeoh was making an example out of me. Instead, he turned to the class and said, "this is what we in the science community need more of … someone who can help encourage people to act, to change the world, even if it's just through a simple story."

He gave me an A+.

I didn't realize it at the time, but that small gesture of defiance helped me real-ize that sometimes, you need to break the rules. Sometimes, it's the system itself that's broken. It was around the same time that I realized the power of storytelling. All of the world's great civilizations stayed intact, in part, because of the power of storytelling. It's how we learn about others. It's how we preserve our history. It's how we promote the ideals and values of the civilizations we belong to. In that sense, there is no higher calling than being a storyteller.

Pro tip

Abandon your preconceived notions of right and wrong. The world is a big place. Some things are black and white, but it's mostly just a whole lotta gray. If you think you already know it all, don't bother getting on the plane.

Leaving aside the importance of journalism's pillars — things like facts, truth, skepticism, rational inquiry, neutrality, etc. — journalism, at its best, serves as a kind of mirror. It's a chance to show people, "This is who we are. And this is what we're capable of."

When we saw the horrific images of abuse and torture at a U.S. detention facility in Iraq's notorious Abu Ghraib prison, we weren't just seeing a historical event, or a simple item on a newscast. We were seeing the depths that we, as a species, can fall to. The same goes for the iconic images of children running in fear after a Napalm attack in Vietnam, or a vulture stalking the body of an emaciated African child suffering through a famine. Those same tendencies, of hatred, seeking power, humiliation, the fear of others — they exist in each and every one of us. This is what makes journalism so powerful. In telling those stories, we can directly touch the human soul.

At times, it's painful. It's like looking in a mirror and seeing your own ugliness reflected. Nobody wants to see that. But a mirror is what it is — a reflection of reality. It's only by seeing humanity's darkness that we can learn to appreciate and cultivate the light. It requires commitment, sacrifice and a relentless ambition to make the world a better place. Without journalists, we wouldn't know about Abu Ghraib, the Nazis' secret human experiments, Napoleon's blitzkrieg into North Africa, or even the trial of Socrates. These are all events that changed the course of history, and we know about them because someone worked hard to document what was happening, and preserve those stories for later generations.

None of this is to say the profession is without its pitfalls. Actually, it's filled with them. There's tons of stuff they'll never teach you in J-School — about ridiculous deadlines, intra-newsroom politics, the dumbing down of content, corporate influences, bad managers who work to sabotage your career, latching on to each new platform as though they're all game changers … the list goes on. If you can somehow survive all that — and make no mistake, it requires a

relentless ambition — the end result is an opportunity to change the world, for your life to have meaning beyond the mundane nine-to-five work culture in the Western world, and to leave some sort of lasting legacy through your words and actions.

It's not for everyone. There will be moments you wished you never read this book by Professor Chimbel and instead took your parents' advice and enrolled into med school. But if you're one of the lucky ones, it'll take you on an amazing journey of discovery where your soul will grow in ways that you can't imagine.

And along the way, hopefully you'll make time for milk and wafers.

Bio

Muhammad Lila is an international correspondent for CNN. He specializes in covering live breaking news in hostile environments. He flies to cool places, meets amazing people and creates multiplatform content.

Before CNN he was a correspondent at ABC News, where he was the only correspondent to file for all ABC News platforms, including "Good Morning America," "World News" and "Nightline" — plus ESPN, Fusion and Yahoo Originals.

He averages 100+ flights a year, has been to the frontlines of nearly every major conflict over the past three years, and received the distinction of being given a personal audience at the home of His Holiness the Dalai Lama. He was also a fill-in anchor for ABC's "World News Now," broadcast out of New York. He once rapped an entire newscast to a Snoop/Dre track. It was wicked fun.

Prior to joining ABC News, Lila was an anchor and reporter for CBC News, based in Toronto, where he became one of the youngest to ever anchor the CBC's flagship newscast, "The National." Prior to that, he was an anchor and reporter for CityTV and CP24, Toronto's top-rated news channel.

Born and raised in Toronto, Lila's background spans three continents. He is fluent in English, conversational in Hindi/Urdu, and continues to study classical Arabic.

He is a graduate of the Graduate School of Journalism at Columbia University. In his spare time, he is an avid travel writer.

Career timeline

2015–present, international correspondent for CNN.
2012–2015, correspondent and anchor at ABC News.
2008–2011, anchor and correspondent at CBC News.
2005–2007, anchor, reporter and editor at CityTV and CP24 in Toronto.
2003, graduated from the Columbia University Graduate School of Journalism.

ROBYN KRIEL

Correspondent

CNN

You hear the phrase "the pen is mightier than the sword" bandied about in various political science and journalism courses with numerous examples throughout history. As a young journalist with two years of experience in local news in the United States, I never thought I would be witness to such a stark example of how true the phrase really is.

In April 2008, I was a general assignment reporter at the CBS affiliate in Waco, Texas. It was my first job out of university and I loved it. But I yearned for home, which was for me the town of Bulawayo, in the southern African nation of Zimbabwe. I was born and raised there, but traveled to the USA for university and then got my first job in local news at KWTX-TV covering Central Texas. Two years into the job, I was transfixed and extremely concerned watching Zimbabwe spiral into chaos from far away. Worried about my family, who still lived there, and with aspirations of being an international correspondent, I was desperate to go home to report on the situation there. I convinced my colleague and best friend, photojournalist Adolfo Ibarra, an American, to join me, and took unpaid leave from KWTX to travel to Zimbabwe and try my hand at reporting international news. We spent our final paychecks on airline tickets and arrived in Zimbabwe to cover the highly contested and dangerous presidential elections just in time to spend Easter with my family.

Looking back now, it was, for both of us, the toughest assignment of our careers and we had very little experience. The Zimbabwean government had launched a huge crackdown on press and media. Most international journalists were not granted permission to report in the country, and by reporting without a permit journalists risked facing 20 years in jail. President Robert Mugabe and his government and police force had a history of civil rights abuses and quite simply didn't want anyone there documenting what would be the most closely contested election in Zimbabwe's history. And with hyperinflation, a huge unemployment rate, massive electoral abuses, political killings, beatings and jailings, there were plenty of stories to tell.

Our work began immediately. We were thrown into the world of undercover reporting — interviewing political activists in secret, keeping their identities hidden and covering with hidden cameras peaceful protests that were violently interrupted by police. As one of the few international broadcasting teams in the country, there was tremendous interest in our reports from CNN, NPR and other outlets, and we couldn't believe how thrilling and adrenaline-filled the world of international news was.

That was until 3 a.m. on April 10, when dozens of armed policemen surrounded our house demanding to know "where the foreign media was." We hid Adolfo in the roof for hours as they searched the property and interrogated my family and I. Eventually he and I were able to escape, after which the police arrested my mother because they mistakenly thought she was the journalist.

They kept her in jail for five days as Adolfo and I were shipped from safe house to safe house before we could leave the country. I was horrified. We weren't murderers, why did it take 20 policemen, setting up roadblocks up and down our street, to arrest a couple of journalists? What were they so very afraid of? And why lock someone in jail for no reason with so little investigation or evidence?

That's when I realized that you can be a dictator with all the guns in the world and a huge army to act on your command, but someone telling the truth — even if she is just a five foot one inch reporter with all of two years' experience — can be a huge, terrifying problem. My mother eventually got out of jail, it was the worst five days of my life, but I was hooked. And that is why I am a journalist.

Pro tip

A photographer in Texas once told me: "If there's coffee, drink it. If there's a bathroom, use it." I swear this is some of the best advice I have ever received and I use it in the field every day.

There is a thing called news karma. It is very real. Always be nice and help a fellow journalist out, even a competitor. You never know when you need news karma on your side. Be nice to interns.

Always be ready for breaking news. Always. It may be the biggest story of your life, your opportunity to shine and propel you to your next career jump, but it will NEVER come at a convenient time. Be ready for it. Have your A-game, a good outfit, comfy shoes and a charged cellphone ready to go. And a charged external battery pack. Maybe two of these.

Always answer your phone and respond to emails promptly. Always.

Eight years on from then and the reasons I love my job are still the same, except I love it even more now. I love flying into a warzone and not knowing what to expect. It is daunting yet hugely exciting. Interviewing victims of war crimes, or the criminals themselves, is hugely important, and there is nothing better than shedding light on a little known story of injustice, of informing the public of something that, if you weren't there to document it, they would not know anything about it.

It's a job that is so vivid and real, yet often so unbelievable, that it rarely feels like a job and often more like a movie — with moments of tragedy mixed in with moments of absolute hilarity.

Some days, though, it's very quiet, bordering on mundane, and you yearn for the thrill of breaking news, of throwing together your "go" bag and heading to the airport, of going live in the field, of arguing with a customs official about your camera equipment, or negotiating a terrifying roadblock. You miss that feeling of jumping into a convoy and heading to an area that you have no idea what

to expect, of sharing a look with your photographer of "what the hell just happened?" and trying to roll with the punches.

And, the best feeling of all, the exhilaration and pride of your story making it to air, despite all the technical and logistical difficulties of a looming deadline, being separated from your equipment because the helicopter carrying the bags ran out of fuel, being yelled at by officials who don't want you to park your van there, of editing as your laptop is running out of battery and there is no electricity, yet you make it with minutes (sometimes seconds) to spare, send the story via satellite to headquarters and then can kick back and watch it play out perfectly edited, beautifully shot, with words that match the pictures.

Your team becomes your family in the field. You eat together, sometimes you have to share rooms, share clothes, share personal sadness or jokes that no one else will ever find funny. You don't have to say a word to each other to know what you are all thinking. And it's a bond that is hard to break. I am still good friends with all of my cameramen nearly a decade later and was part of Adolfo's wedding.

At times you can get bogged down with the technical aspects of the job. Such as why a live shot didn't work out, or why this government won't let us broadcast live from this event, or why you aren't allowed to do this story that you find important but are asked to focus on another. We, at times, forget that our jobs can be so important, particularly those for whom free press is not a reality, or those who desperately need their stories told to make change. We also can forget just how much fun the job is. We are witnessing history. We are doing things that so few people will ever get to do and our days are never the same. My first story for local news was covering a mass wedding at the McLennan County Courthouse in downtown Waco on Valentine's Day. Later that day I covered a tragedy where someone had slipped off a cliff at the park and died. A decade later I'm covering a famine in Somalia and a few months after that I'm on a safari story keeping up with the Great Migration deep in the heart of Kenya's Maasai Mara. It is such a privilege to tell those stories. To be invited into people's homes, and lives, and for them to allow us to film during their most special day, or their very worst nightmare. I am thankful for every day I am out in the field, a photographer and producer at my side, the best of the best, allowed to do my job. That is why I am a journalist, and I love every minute of it.

Bio

Robyn Kriel is an award-winning correspondent and anchor for CNN. A journalist with a wealth of experience, Kriel has covered major news stories across Africa.

Kriel reported on President Barack Obama's 2015 visit to East Africa, U.S. Secretary of State John Kerry's visit to Somalia and the discovery of the MH370 debris on Reunion Island.

Prior to joining CNN in 2015, Kriel served as chief Africa correspondent for South African news broadcaster eNCA. While working at eNCA, Kriel traveled extensively across East Africa — contributing to major stories, including the war and drought in Somalia, cross border clashes along the Sudan/South Sudan border, hostages held by pirates rescued in Puntland, the Westgate Mall attack in Nairobi and the Garissa University attacks in northeast Kenya.

Kriel's early career was spent covering Zimbabwe's economic and political meltdown. This included the 2007 price control crisis, the state crackdown on media and civil society groups and the 2008 March elections.

Kriel's career has also taken her outside of Africa. In 2010, she traveled to Afghanistan, where she spent a month embedded with U.S. Marines in Helmand Province covering the Afghan parliamentary elections.

Throughout her career, Kriel has won a number of reporting accolades including an Edward R. Murrow Award for in-depth series reporting, an Overseas Press Club honorable mention, a David Burke Award for Bravery in Journalism, a Houston Press Club Award and two Lone Star Emmys. In 2011, Kriel was recognized by Michelle Obama for what the First Lady called her "courageous reporting from Zimbabwe."

Born and raised in Zimbabwe, Kriel graduated from TCU in Fort Worth, Texas, with degrees in broadcast journalism and musical theater. She is currently completing her Master of Arts in war studies through a distance-learning program at King's College London.

Career timeline

2016–present, weekend CNN anchor based in Atlanta.

2015–2016, East Africa correspondent for CNN.

2011–2015, chief correspondent for Africa for eNCA in Nairobi.

2008–2011, anchor and reporter for eNCA in Johannesburg, South Africa.

2006–2008, general assignment reporter for KWTX-TV in Waco, Texas.

December 2005, graduated from TCU with majors in broadcast journalism and musical theater.

CAN DÜNDAR

Former editor-in-chief of the Cumhuriyet newspaper

Turkey

Source: © Claude Truong-Ngoc

It's a very simple question: If you knew you could go to prison over a sentence you were about to write, would you still write it?

I took this test in May 2015. My newspaper, the Cumhuriyet, had, for the past few months, been reporting how Turkey had become a willing thoroughfare for fighters and weapons to radical Islamists in Syria. Finally, we obtained a terrific video documenting the claims. It revealed that trucks intercepted by a branch of the Turkish military, the Gendarmes (and identified as belonging to the Turkish Intelligence Service), were transporting weapons and munitions under a layer of boxes of medicines.

This was an international crime. One serious enough to send the culprits to the international courts ... Needless to say, the report was as important as the risk of publishing was great. Especially in a land like Turkey, where the freedom of the press is so easily trampled upon and journalists are so easily banged up.

We convened an editorial meeting straight away and invited our counselors too. Not surprisingly, their legal concerns dampened our journalistic fervor somewhat: publishing could lead to the government seizing the papers on grounds of disclosing state secrets, and arresting the writer. Their final advice was, "Your call."

A journalist's dilemma: On the one hand, the thrill of a bombshell news item, and on the other, the risk of prison.

The dream and the nightmare.

That's when I wondered, "Why am I a journalist?"

I'd read journalism for four years, then carried on training in London. By a strange coincidence, my master's thesis was on state secrets and freedom of the press. I'd been a journalist for 35 years. One thing I'd learned was that our job is to defend the public's right to know, not the government's interests.

When we receive information, we check two things:

1   Is it true?
2   Is it in the public's interest to publish it?

The report was true, and the public had a right to know.

What if it was dangerous to publish the report? The responsibility there was to take the risk.

We all knew — from the off — that reporting was not an easy job in Turkey. Our role models when we were undergraduates were either in prison or in the grave. Five columnists from my paper, the Cumhuriyet, had been assassinated. The entrance to our building was covered with their portraits and the headlines that had caused their deaths. In a manner of speaking, every day we were saluting this bloodied banner we had taken over.

Truth was a fortress that had to be conquered, even at the risk of life, a fortress that we had to conquer, even if it were emblazoned with nationalist flags at the entrance. This endeavor gained even more importance in a place like Turkey, where seeking the truth exacts a heavy price.

Talent alone wasn't enough to be a journalist; you needed courage too. Without that courage, today, we would have been ignorant of Watergate and Irangate. Neither WikiLeaks nor the Panama Papers would have leaked. Yet they all had been unearthed by journalists who answer the question, "Why am I a journalist?" with, "To uncover the truth."

They had toppled presidents at times and thrown up dirty deals at others. If a government busy pouring petrol on its neighbor's fire, thereby endangering its own nation, wanted to sweep its own secrets under a carpet called "state secrets," our job was to lift that carpet.

"All right," I said, "We run with it."

As predicted, the next day our website shared the video and was censored. The prosecutor started an enquiry against me straight away. In the evening, the then-Prime Minister Recep Tayyip Erdoğan openly threatened me on a live TV program: "The person who published this report will pay a heavy price. I'm not letting him go that easily."

This statement was the first harbinger of the prices I would have to pay one after the other. The court waited until after the election before the arrest.

Erdoğan admitted to the munitions in the trucks after he'd won: "So they claim there were munitions in the lorries. So what?"

Three weeks later, our Ankara bureau chief, Erdem Gül, and I were arrested. His "crime" was publishing the inventory of the weapons captured in the trucks.

We would be tried on four charges:

1   Divulging secret official documents.
2   Aiding and abetting an armed organization.
3   Espionage.
4   Attempting to topple the government.

What the prosecution sought for one single news item, one that was true at that, was a double life sentence — equivalent to capital punishment in the old criminal law. In other words, they were seeking the death penalty for a factual news item.

It was my first time in jail. In November 2015, in solitary confinement in Turkey's biggest prison, I was in a cold cell, when I asked myself the same question again: "Why am I a journalist?"

We were the hunters of a treasure called truth. We had to reveal it, digging patiently with a fine-tipped pen like an archaeologist if need be. What we were digging with that pen could be our own cell or grave. Who cares! That was par for the course. The shame of staying silent or failing to write would have been far worse than the price we were paying.

I decided to carry on writing in the cell. There was no computer, and typewriters were banned. All I had was pen and paper. So I wrote. I flooded all the newspapers of the world I knew of; I yelled the truth I learned so they could hear.

Inmates were forbidden to send their writing out without the warden's knowledge. But a reporter raised in a land of prohibitions knows how to circumvent them. I managed to get my articles over to my colleagues who stood on the Vigil of Hope outside the prison and to the leading publications of the West. What the government was trying to keep secret was heard around the world.

The price of journalism had won recognition. I couldn't see the world, but I could feel that the world was seeing me. After a three-month period of detention, we were released by a Constitutional Court order. But the trial continued.

The counsel for Erdoğan (now president) and the National Intelligence Service sat in the plaintiffs' chairs. The judge asked: "You're accused of reporting state secrets that should have remained a secret. Why did you do it?"

That vital question confronted me once again: "Why was I a journalist?"

Because I knew that the government must not be the sole authority to decide what could be known, and what could not. Otherwise the concept of "secrets" could be used to cover up official crimes. My news item was the perfect example. What was in question was not a state secret, but the secret of the government of the time. And an international crime was being swept under the carpet. In case the government's need to hide and the public's right to know clashed, which one would we defend?

Naturally the public's right to know. That was our raison d'être as journalists.

I presented my defense and the judges retired to deliberate. We went outside to wait. In the most tightly guarded square in Istanbul, right outside the courthouse, a man was rushing toward me. Then a barely noticeable flash, a sudden smell of gunpowder and a yell that accompanied the bang: "Traitor!"

This was the term Erdoğan had been trying to ascribe to me; someone had volunteered to extract the price he had demanded. I was spared thanks to the courage of my wife who grabbed that gunman's arm.

We then returned to the courtroom to hear the verdict: "Five years and 10 months for divulging state secrets."

I had suffered two assassinations within an hour, one physical, and the other judicial. I announced to my fellow journalists gathered at the exit that we would never be silenced.

Where journalists turn a deaf ear and keep silent, society goes deaf and dumb.

Today, I live away from my homeland. The government has issued an arrest warrant for me. My assailant has been released after five months in prison; but my wife, who faces no charges, has been taken hostage: her passport was confiscated at the airport with no explanation and she was stopped from going abroad.

I have lost my freedom, my home, my job, my wife, my country, all for an item of news. My life was in danger.

Was it worth it?

Let's go back to the beginning. If you're a journalist in a country like Turkey, where there is no freedom of the press, you know which sentence can send you to prison and which news item can kill you. One word could put you in someone's gun sight; one cartoon could cause your home to be bombed.

When you join this profession, you do it with your eyes open. Either choose the easy way and join the pro-government media or learn to live with danger.

As 2017 begins, in Turkey nearly 150 journalists are in prison, 2,500 journalists are out of a job, 150 media outlets including newspapers, TV and radio stations and magazines are shut down and social media is under government control; this makes Turkey the greatest prison for journalists today.

The reason is the fury of the government frightened of the truth, and the courage of journalists undaunted by the government.

Today, as I live far from my country, my home, my family and my newspaper, I continue writing the truth and screaming it out as I know it, and I ask myself: "Why am I a journalist?"

The answer is simple: To defend the truth. Lands where the truth is not defended are condemned to live with lies. And the path to dictatorship is paved with lies.

Bio

Can Dündar is the former editor-in-chief of the Turkish daily newspaper Cumhuriyet. He was sentenced to five years and 10 months in prison on charges of revealing state secrets for reporting by his paper, which he is appealing.

The Committee to Protect Journalists honored him with one of its 2016 International Press Freedom Awards.

Prior to joining Cumhuriyet as its top editor in 2015, Dündar worked for several newspapers in Turkey, produced documentaries and worked on television programs.

Dündar studied at Ankara University, the London School of Journalism and the Middle Eastern Technical University, where he earned a Ph.D. in political science.

He is currently living in Germany.

Media journalists

Journalists are natural gossips. It's sort of inherently in a reporter's DNA to find out what's going on and tell people about it.

Journalists love to talk about their industry, too, and the broader media landscape it operates within — and for good reason. Media is a dominant part of our lives.

Multiple studies of Americans' use of media show we average 10 hours or more a day with media, a number that is increasing and we are constantly connected via our smart, compact and personal devices.

We spend more than time, too. By some estimates Americans spend more money on media than clothing and health care combined. Advertisers spend billions of dollars a year to get their messages to you.

Think about your day and your spending. What do you do with your time and how do you spend your money?

That mass of media, however, is increasingly concentrated. In the 1980s, about 90 percent of the media was controlled by 50 companies, but now it's down to just six after a series of mergers and acquisitions over the past 30 years.

Keeping an eye on those companies is part of the watchdog role of journalism, and the journalists who cover media represent an increasingly important part of our field, but it also comes with inherent conflicts because these journalists are tasked with covering their industry and competitors, and sometimes their own news organizations.

Works cited

Baran, S.J. (2011). Introduction to Mass Communication: Media Literacy and Culture (7th edn). New York: McGraw-Hill.

Bauder, D. (2016, June 29). Media use in America up a full hour over just last year. Associated Press.

Chimbel, A. (2014). Introduction to Journalism (2nd edn). Dubuque, IA: Kendall Hunt.

ERIC DEGGANS

Television critic

NPR

This might be the main reason why I became a journalist: It's in my blood.

My father, Charles Milton Deggans, was a longtime columnist for several newspapers in my hometown of Gary, Ind., including black-focused publications like Gary INFO and the Gary Crusader, along with the big newspaper in town, the Post-Tribune.

My dad's column — artfully titled "Deggans' Den" — came along in the 1960s, when newspapers would publish social columns of a sort; a collection of all the parties, fundraisers and big events in town, with photos and shout-outs to everyone who was anyone. In the Post-Tribune especially, my dad was the man who brought the city's black social scene to the newspaper, covering all the hip parties and events, spiced with photos of cute women in bikinis in the manner of old school magazines like Jet.

It was a bit like Gary's black-centered, sanitized print version of the Playboy Club; there was even a graphic with the column that featured my dad in a cool pose. It was a place in the newspaper to find out where the city's coolest people were doing the coolest things. And it was a column that everybody knew.

I still remember visiting the set of the syndicated TV show "Star Trek: Deep Space Nine" as I was building my career as a TV critic. I had snagged an interview with its famously press-averse star Avery Brooks, who probably only agreed to speak with me because he was also from Gary. His first question, asked from behind the barely-cracked-open door of his trailer: "Your daddy write 'Deggans Den?'" When I said "yes," he smiled and the interview began.

It was a particular point of pride for me that, when I was in high school in the early 1980s, I wrote a column about my school in the very same newspaper my dad columnized for, Gary INFO. And even though my columns read very differently — I tried to tell sophisticated stories with a bit of voice, like my early writing heroes, Stan Lee and Mike Royko — I knew on some level my impulse to write for an audience came from him, a least a little bit.

But I was also pragmatic. I knew I could write. I knew I could play music as a budding drummer. I knew I could draw a bit, but not well enough to develop it as a profession. So I asked myself, as a sophomore in high school: What could I do that would bring together my love of music with my love of writing and earn a steady paycheck?

My answer might amuse those who actually try to make a living doing it now: I wanted to work as a pop music critic for a national news outlet.

I worked hard to learn the language of pop music criticism from that moment on, devouring copies of Vibe, Rolling Stone, Spin, Musician, Playboy (yes, it really did have great articles on pop music and other stuff back then), the Village Voice (although that stuff was a little too urban and sophisticated for me back then) and even Modern Drummer magazine. I had no idea how to get a job at any of those places, but I soaked up how they talked about music.

Pro tip

Be flexible. Be focused. Be reliable. Be adventurous. Be creative. Be ethical.

There's a famous quote, at times attributed to performers like Martin Mull and Elvis Costello: "writing about music is like dancing about architecture." It's a statement I'm sure was meant to tweak critics a bit. But whoever said it had a point; the process of describing music is so abstract, you often have to learn from the language of those who have done it before. What's the best way to describe how James Brown drummer John "Jabo" Starks hits a muscular rimshot? How to deploy words in a way to evoke the lush jangle of Prince's guitar in the poignant beginning to "Purple Rain"? My answer was to gorge on the words of those who had already figured it out, and then try those techniques in my own work.

I was learning all that and more in my self-imposed apprenticeship, which stretched into my college years. Back in the mid-1980s, the biggest challenge for aspiring writers in the pre-internet age was getting published, so I wrote for any outlet that would publish my work while majoring in journalism and political science at Indiana University.

When you're in your late teens and using college to figure out your future, it's easy to be oblivious. So I don't think I realized back then just how lucky I was: IU's main campus in Bloomington, Ind. housed one of the country's top journalism schools. And this Gary native got to attend paying a lower, in-state tuition, with a modest scholarship thrown in.

IU was also home to one of the country's best music schools. And while participating in an elective class through the Afro-American Studies department called the IU Soul Review — musicians, singers and dancers recreated the history of African-Americans in a concert performance — I met a group of musicians who would change my life, both as a journalist and a performer.

We gathered in a dormitory on IU's campus, hoping to pull together a band to make some pocket money on the side and maybe write some songs. We picked what we thought was an original name: Voyage (after our marathon naming session, a dorm buddy heard the result and asked "Is that anything like Journey?" Argh.) Our story might be worth an essay all its own; but within a few years, we had narrowly avoided breaking up by writing a hit song that made a big splash on a local charity record and eventually got signed to Motown Records.

The Motown experience was mostly disappointing. Not long after we got signed, owner/founder Berry Gordy began positioning the company for a sale, which happened about a year after we joined the roster. Most acts, including us, got dropped. But I learned valuable lessons for my future as a journalist and pop culture critic; what it feels and looks like to be a band on the verge of getting released by a major label.

I also inherited a need to explain how this world worked to fans who generally had no clue. I'll never forget the time our band opened up our process to a student who was writing a feature story for the school newspaper, and proceeded to make every journalism mistake possible. This fledgling reporter talked to managers we had just fired without telling us or giving us a chance to respond to their allegations, while also misspelling the names of half the people in the group. I vowed that when I was writing about this stuff as a professional in the real world, I'd work hard to make sure no subject felt as unfairly burned as we were by that piece.

So my dad and my time as a professional musician pushed me toward work as an arts and pop culture critic, for different reasons. But there was a third and final influence that I have come to recognize only in recent years.

You may have noticed earlier in this essay that I referenced the great Stan Lee. Some younger folks may only know him as the weird old dude with a moustache who gets a cameo in every Marvel superhero movie (he is carried out by two guys after drinking too much with "Thor in Avengers: Age of Ultron," for example).

But for us lifelong comic book geeks, he was the guy who really revolutionized comics so the storytelling could entertain adults and stand as important media platforms in the modern age. Yes, he created or co-created many of the Marvel superheroes you now see in film and TV, including Spider-Man, Hulk, Iron Man, Daredevil, Thor and the X-Men. And if he'd only done that, his place in the storytelling hall of fame would be secure.

But what he really did, partnered with amazing artists like Steve Ditko and Jack Kirby, was create a comic book world that was more realistic, relevant and diverse than the universe populated by Marvel's biggest competition, DC (home to Superman, Batman, Wonder Woman and the Flash, among others).

Stan Lee's heroes lived in real places like Queens and Hell's Kitchen, not Metropolis or Gotham City. They used slang that made fans feel like members of an exclusive club (Google Lee's name and the word "excelsior." Trust me.) They could feel vaguely ethnic — and at times included black superheroes like Black Panther and Luke Cage — when DC's heroes felt bland as a scoop of vanilla ice cream.

As a kid who was often bullied in my neighborhood — bestowed with thick glasses in the first grade, my nickname was "The Professor" — comic books offered a fantasy world where powerful beings made sure justice was done. And only now do I realize that they also sparked a thirst for justice that has spilled over into my professional life.

There is no greater pleasure for me professionally than calling out inequality, injustice or a scam. Sometimes it's a story in the St. Petersburg Times revealing that a guy about to get the key to the city is actually just pretending to be a Grammy-award winning singer, other times, it's a pointed conversation with CBS executives about why every new TV series they debuted in fall 2016 starred white male characters.

Throughout my career, I've seen myself as a surrogate for the audience and a voice against deceit, unfairness and unethical behavior. I hate most unscripted "reality TV" shows because they are never honest with the audience about how producers affect the scenes we see; as a local media columnist, I criticized local TV stations for dangerous stunts like parking a Ryder truck near a federal building in Tampa, Fla. on the first day of the prosecution of Oklahoma City bomber Timothy McVeigh. The trial was in Colorado, but the Tampa station wanted to test security on the other side of the country in our town — no matter how much it freaked out police officers who weren't aware it was a hoax.

Even now, I view a big part of my job as a TV critic in the simplest terms: To cut through the spin and nonsense of the television industry, giving people an unvarnished sense of what they are watching and why it's being served to them. It's about handing the audience the tools to be their own superheroes — pushing back against the spin, stereotypical images, materialism, sexism, classism and consumerism embedded in so much media today.

To be honest, when I began to focus on building a journalism career, I always thought my big job would be in print, at The New York Times, Washington Post, Rolling Stone or some other storied publication. But opportunity for me came in a different area, and as I write this, I'm bringing coverage of television to a media outlet that never had a full-time TV critic until I started working there: NPR, once known as National Public Radio.

Another observation I have about this moment in the industry: I started out as a generalist developing reports for a very specific news outlet — I was a suburban news reporter in Pittsburgh, covering all types of news in six different school districts for the Pittsburgh Press newspaper. Now, I'm a journalist with a very specific coverage area — TV and pop culture — generating material for a wide range of media platforms, including radio, online, magazines or newspapers (as a freelancer) or through TV appearances.

The change reveals how technology has opened up new opportunities for journalists willing to work on different platforms, especially if they have an area of expertise that can produce good stories in all those spaces.

Overall, I believe I became a journalist — and remain one as I write this — because I wanted to tell stories that made a difference. Who knew the road to that reality would run through Rolling Stone, Motown Records, Stan Lee and "Deggans' Den"?

R.I.P. dad. Hope I'm still making you proud.

Bio

Eric Deggans is NPR's first full-time TV critic, crafting stories and commentaries for the network's shows, such as "Morning Edition," "Here & Now" and "All Things Considered," along with writing material for NPR.org and the website's blogs such as Code Switch, Monkey See and The Two Way. He came to NPR in September 2013 from the Tampa Bay Times newspaper in Florida, where he served as TV/media critic and in other roles for nearly 20 years. A journalist for more than two decades, he is also the author of "Race-Baiter: How the Media Wields Dangerous Words to Divide a Nation," a look at how prejudice, racism and sexism fuels some elements of modern media, published in October 2012 by Palgrave Macmillan.

He guest hosted CNN's media analysis show "Reliable Sources" several times in fall 2013, joining a select group of journalists and media critics filling in for departed host Howard Kurtz. That year, he also earned the Florida Press Club's first-ever Diversity Award, honoring his coverage of issues involving race and media. He has received Legacy Awards from both the Tampa Bay Association of Black Journalists and the National Association of Black Journalists' A&E Task Force. The NABJ's award was an honor bestowed to "seasoned A&E journalists who are at the top of their careers." Eric also serves on the board of educators, journalists and media experts who select the George Foster Peabody Awards for excellence in electronic media.

He also has joined a prestigious group of contributors to the first ethics book created in a partnership between Craigslist founder Craig Newmark and the Poynter Institute for Media Studies. Developed as Poynter's first ethics book for the digital age, The New Ethics of Journalism was published in August 2013 by SAGE/CQ Press. Deggans has also been named a distinguished alumnus of Indiana University, featured in their Luminaries program in late 2015.

Named in 2009 as one of Ebony magazine's "Power 150" — a list of influential black Americans which also included Oprah Winfrey and PBS host Gwen Ifill — Deggans was selected to lecture at Columbia University's prestigious Graduate School of Journalism in 2005 and 2008. In November 2015, he spent several days lecturing at Indiana University as part of its IU Luminaries program, in which students choose notable alumni to return for a three-day visit. He has also lectured or taught as an adjunct professor at DePaul University, Loyola University, George Washington University, California State University, University of Tampa, Eckerd College and many other colleges.

He has served as keynote speaker for several groups, including the Florida Library Association, the National High School Journalism Association and the International Communication Association, along with moderating a panel with producers and stars of "The Walking Dead" series for the Smithsonian.

His writing has also appeared in The New York Times online, Salon magazine, CNN.com, The Washington Post, Village Voice, Vibe magazine, Chicago Tribune, Detroit Free Press, Chicago Sun-Times, Chicago Tribune,

Seattle Times, Emmy magazine, Newsmax magazine, Rolling Stone online and a host of other newspapers across the country.

From 2004 to 2005, he sat on the then St. Petersburg Times editorial board and wrote bylined opinion columns. From1997 to 2004, he worked as TV critic for the Times, crafting reviews, news stories and long-range trend pieces on the state of the media industry both locally and nationally. He originally joined the paper as its pop music critic in November 1995; he has also worked at the Asbury Park Press in New Jersey and both the Pittsburgh Post-Gazette and Pittsburgh Press newspapers in Pennsylvania.

Now serving as co-chair of the Media Monitoring Committee for the National Association of Black Journalists, he has also served on the board of directors for the national Television Critics Association and on the board of the Mid-Florida Society of Professional Journalists.

Additionally, he worked as a professional drummer in the 1980s, touring and performing with Motown recording artists The Voyage Band throughout the Midwest and in Osaka, Japan. He continues to perform with area bands and recording artists as a drummer, bassist and vocalist.

Career timeline

2013–present, TV critic for NPR.

2005–2013, television/media critic at the Tampa Bay Times/St. Petersburg Times.

2004–2005, columnist and editorial board member at the St. Petersburg Times.

1996–2004, television/media critic at the St. Petersburg Times.

1995–1996, pop music critic at the St. Petersburg Times.

1993–1995, music writer at the Asbury Park Press in New Jersey.

1993, reporter at the Pittsburgh Post-Gazette.

May 1990, graduated from the Indiana University School of Journalism.

BRIAN STELTER

Senior media correspondent and host of "Reliable Sources"

CNN

In 1996, when I was 11 years old, I was motivated to learn HTML code and create a website about a children's book series called "Goosebumps." Why? Well the way I remember it, I was obsessed with the books and I couldn't find a great website that would answer all my questions. So I created the website that I wanted to read. The Bumps connected a community of "Goosebumps" fans across the country.

The same reasoning propelled me to start a blog about television news from my college dorm room in 2004. TVNewser eventually reached millions of people.

And the same thing motivates me at CNN now. Having questions. Seeking an audience that shares those questions. Finding the answers.

In between The Bumps and CNN were more websites, more blogs, internships, school newspapers and a coveted job at The New York Times — untold thousands of stories, blog posts, late nights and early mornings. But in my mind, I can draw a pretty straight line between that 11-year-old coder and the 31-year-old anchor who's writing this now.

At CNN, I report on the wide world of media and host a weekly program called "Reliable Sources." Every week I introduce the program by calling it "our weekly look at the story behind the story, of how the media REALLY works, how the news gets made." Basically I cover journalism and the other journalists who contributed to this book.

I approach my job like it is a four-legged stool, each leg essential to holding the rest together. The first leg is daily reporting and writing for CNN's digital properties. The second leg is appearing on TV throughout the week, sharing my reporting on CNN shows like "New Day" and "Anderson Cooper 360." The third leg is "Reliable Sources," on Sunday mornings, the end of one week and the start of a new week. And the fourth leg is a nightly newsletter, also called "Reliable Sources," that summarizes the other three legs and promotes CNN's growing team of media and entertainment reporters.

There is a big audience for this coverage because media is intertwined with so many other subjects — including politics, foreign affairs, business, sports and culture. I find that thousands of people write about the media, opine about it, complain about it … but a much smaller number of people actually report on it. When you find a space like that, it's an opportunity.

Pro tip

Try to be indispensable, own a beat and develop an expertise call about a subject, location or platform.

Wherever there are more questions than answers. Wherever demand for information outstrips supply. That's a good place for a beat.

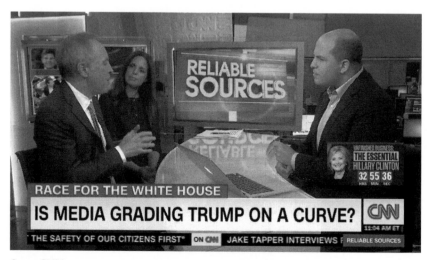

Source: CNN

What I was doing back in the mid-1990s wasn't journalism, per se, the way I know it today, but it was journalistic. The Bumps was a fan website, cataloging past "Goosebumps" books, printing trivia questions, looking ahead to the next book in the series, etcetera. The Bumps spawned imitators — other kids who also loved the books and loved learning HTML — but I was determined to be the "#1 Goosebumps site." That was my immodest slogan.

I kept the site going for years, and eventually I became pen pals with the author of "Goosebumps," R.L. Stine, and his son Matt. Now we're real-life friends. When I interviewed Stine on my program in 2015, he recalled "going to your website every day to find out what was happening with 'Goosebumps.'" He laughed. "You were such an aggressive 12-year-old! I mean, you would call Steven Spielberg and say, what's happening with the 'Goosebumps' DVD game? And you would call Scholastic," the publisher of the series.

I never called what I was doing "reporting," but that's what it was. The invention of the Internet allowed me — like everyone else with a modem — to become a publisher. When I grew out of "Goosebumps" books, I started websites about Nintendo games and Xbox games, like a cub reporter moving from one neighborhood to another.

Looking back now, my obsession with media was obvious in all sorts of ways. I printed out wire copy and anchored homemade newscasts in the basement. I called in snowfall totals to my local TV stations. I ran the high school paper and the weekly in-school TV newscast. Sometimes I was just informing thousands of people, other times just a handful. But if you've ever had a byline, you know the real thrill isn't seeing your name in print, but seeing someone learn something from your story.

What I'm describing entailed thousands of hours of unpaid work. It was fun — but it was done for free. TVNewser came about because I was felt like no one was reporting enough detail about the daily battles of the cable news wars. I was fascinated by the on- and off-screen maneuverings of Fox News, CNN and MSNBC. I thought that other people cared too — and the traffic to the blog proved this. Once again, creating the website that I wanted to read was the path to success.

The Times hired me in 2007 largely thanks to the blog, although I hasten to add that I also needed my Towson University journalism degree and years of experience editing a college newspaper. Even with all that, the first few months were a struggle. I knew how to be a blogger, but not quite a "newspaper reporter." I wrote my way to the answer. Every time my editors asked for a story, I said yes. When they didn't ask, I wrote a story anyway. "Fake it until you make it" is clichéd advice that helped me through those months.

Nowadays, the advice I offer is to try to be indispensable. Try to "own" some beat, bring some expertise, be THE person to call about this subject or that location or this platform. This is all a version of supply and demand, right? Be the person with lots of questions and some of the answers. I'm a journalist because our communities are only as well off as the information we have. Right now there is tremendous demand for information and terrific new ways to supply it to people. Wherever you see questions, help supply answers.

Bio

Brian Stelter is the host of "Reliable Sources," which examines the week's top media stories every Sunday at 11 a.m. ET on CNN/U.S., and the senior media correspondent for CNN Worldwide. Stelter reports and writes for CNN and CNNMoney.

Prior to joining CNN in November 2013, Stelter was a media reporter at The New York Times. Starting in 2007, he covered television and digital media for the Business Day and Arts section of the newspaper. He was also a lead contributor to the Media Decoder blog.

In January 2004, while he was still a freshman in college, Stelter created TVNewser, a blog dedicated to coverage of the television news industry. He sold it to Mediabistro.com in July 2004, but continued to edit and write for the blog during the next three years until he graduated college and joined The New York Times.

Stelter published The New York Times best-selling book, "Top of the Morning: Inside the Cutthroat World of Morning TV" (2013), about the competitive world of morning news shows. He was featured in the 2011 documentary, "Page One: Inside the New York Times," directed by Andrew Rossi. He has been named to Forbes Magazine's "30 Under 30: Media" lists for the past three years.

Stelter graduated with a bachelor's degree in mass communications with a concentration in journalism from Towson University in Baltimore, Maryland, in 2007. He is on the board of Baltimore Student Media, a nonprofit that publishes Towson's independent student newspaper, The Towerlight.

Career timeline

2013–present, senior media correspondent and host of "Reliable Sources" at CNN.

2013, published The New York Times best-selling book, "Top of the Morning: Inside the Cutthroat World of Morning TV."

2007–2013, media reporter at The New York Times.

2007, graduated from Towson University with a degree in mass communication.

2004–2007, creator and editor of TVNewser.

KRISTEN HARE

Reporter

Poynter Institute for Media Studies

The first time I got the chance to speak at career day at my son's school, I signed up. I mean, I'm a reporter: I have a really cool job. I knew the kindergartners in Mrs. Flores' class would agree.

What I didn't know was that I'd go right after a dad who was a manager at our neighborhood Sonic, or that he'd bring everyone fries and toys, and that, to kindergartners, that was way cooler.

Still, my son, Max, tried to help me out.

"You guys," he said when it was clear I was tanking after free-fries-dad, "she gets to talk to strangers for a living!"

That helped a bit.

The next year, I signed up again. And this time, I was ready. I got paper rectangles, plastic pockets and black lanyards with the word POYNTER printed around them. And when it was my turn to talk, I pulled out my press pass.

OK it's not really a press pass. It's my work ID. But I wear it around my neck on that same lanyard when I'm reporting, and, I told Mrs. Hensel's first-grade class, it's kind of magic. That pass gets me in places that I couldn't get in otherwise.

It got me into the cab of a trash truck when I was a young reporter, where I spent a day in the life of a garbage collector, I told them. They oohhhed. It got me into the belly of Kauffman Stadium in Kansas City, into the dugout, onto the field, to interview a Kansas City Royals baseball player for a Father's Day story.

They ahhhhed. And, just a few months earlier, it got me into the streets of a city where I went to cover a protest. They oohhhed.

Here's what I didn't tell that class of first-graders: weeks before my son started school, a young black man was shot and killed on the streets of Ferguson, Missouri. About a week later, I took Max to his first day of first grade, took his sister to preschool and headed for Tampa International Airport. I arrived in St. Louis and spent the day reporting at local newsrooms. That night, with a gas mask, a notebook, a pen and my phone, I headed into Ferguson.

But where I needed to go, a stretch of West Florissant Avenue where nightly protests and clashes with heavily armed police unfolded, was blocked off by police. I pulled up and rolled down the window of my rental car. The police waved at me to keep driving.

"I'm media," I said. "Can I get in?"

"You got a press pass?" the officer asked.

I grabbed my ID and that lanyard and gave it to him.

"What's the Poynter Institute?" he asked.

I told him we were a school for journalists, that I covered the media, and that I was there to cover how journalists were covering the story.

He chuckled.

"That should be interesting."

He waved me through.

I wore that ID around my neck both of the long, sweaty nights I spent in Ferguson. It wasn't work that was cool or exciting, like the stuff I'd told my son's class about. It was scary. It was heartbreaking. And being a journalist meant that I was there to see it, to question people there, and to take what I found back to our audience through words and images.

Pro tip

Aim big, start small. You'll learn so much in small, local newsrooms when you're starting out if you look for the opportunities. There are a lot of them. Do your assignments, make them your own, save great stories that may be slightly off your beat and pitch them when your editors are in a really good mood.

I found other journalists in Ferguson because they, too, wore their IDs around their necks. On my last night there, I stopped to talk with an older black man who wore an ID.

"Who do you work for?" I asked Clarence Williams.

He wasn't a journalist, he told me.

"I have to look like the media to protect myself."

He was there, like a lot of us, because he wanted to witness what was happening and he wanted to tell people what he saw. Inside the plastic pocket dangling from the lanyard around his neck was a folded up guide to the Metrolink.

"This," Mr. Williams told me, "allows me to get closer to the story."

Back in Max's class a few months later, I showed his friends my ID. Then, I gave them the paper rectangles, the plastic pockets and the long black lanyards.

What do you want to know more about? I asked them. Where do you want to go? Who do you want to talk to?

They bubbled with ideas: video game designers, Disney World, the Tampa Bay Buccaneers' stadium.

Now draw a box and draw your face inside, I said. Write your name, and then what you report about. This is your press pass, I said.

They loved it, possibly even more than the "she talks to strangers for a living" line, which Max tried again.

Every year since, I've signed up for career day. In Mrs. Gaines' class, in Mrs. Franklin's class, in Mrs. Wintenburg's class, I've told them tales of the places I've been, the people I've met, the questions I've asked and the stories I've told. Every year since, I've brought rectangles of paper, plastic pockets and black lanyards. And every year since, I've thanked the parenting gods that I didn't have to follow Sonic dad again.

I first considered becoming a journalist because my dad told me it was a way to be a writer and pay the bills. I learned to become a journalist because of a high

school journalism teacher whose lessons on free speech and democracy crept into my brain and put down roots. I kept learning in college after that summer creative writing class when all my papers were marked down for using AP style and I realized I could never dream up stories as good as the ones I could find in real life. I became a working journalist after two years and a thousand adventures in the Peace Corps.

And I've stayed a journalist because this job, my notebook, my pen, and that press pass help get me into the places and find the people whose stories need to be told. It might not be free fries, but it still kind of feels like magic.

Bio

Kristen Hare is a media reporter for the Poynter Institute. Before taking on the meta job of covering the industry she's part of, Hare spent five years reporting on race, immigration, aging and the census for the St. Louis Beacon and five years as a Sunday features writer for the St. Joseph News-Press. Hare graduated from the University of Missouri's School of Journalism in 2000, then spent two years in Guyana with the Peace Corps. Hare, who now lives outside Tampa with her family, is also the author of the book "100 Things to do in Tampa Bay Before You Die."

Career timeline

2014, published first book, "100 Things to do in Tampa Bay Before You Die."

2013–present, reporter at the Poynter Institute.

2008–2013, general assignment reporter at the St. Louis Beacon.

2005–2008, assistant features editor at the St. Joseph News-Press.

2005, winner of the Sifford Memorial Prize in Journalism from the University of Missouri.

2003–2005, features reporter, St. Joseph News-Press.

2000, graduated from the University of Missouri School of Journalism.

Business journalists

No matter what you cover as a journalist, it almost always comes down to one thing: money. Politics, government, education, entertainment, technology and even sports all have a lot to do with money and business. It's inescapable.

As it turns out, it makes sense then that business and financial journalism is one of the strongest parts of the industry.

The Wall Street Journal consistently ranks as one of the top three newspapers in the country and was well ahead of many of its print counterparts by implementing a paywall for its website shortly after the site launched more than 20 years ago, charging for its business-focused news while other newspapers were giving content away for free.

A seemingly endless number of publications and digital news organizations cover the intersection of business and technology, personal finance and investing. Issues of money affect us all and we want to know what to do with what we have.

Cable news channels CNBC, Fox Business and Bloomberg all provide 24/7 financial news, too.

There is a particular challenge, however, to covering business that is not necessarily the same as for other journalists. When you cover government entities such as legislatures and school boards, reporters benefit from state and federal sunshine laws, meaning matters of public importance are accessible to the public through open meetings and public records requests, providing an important window into what is going on. However, when you cover private businesses, you don't have that benefit and must gather information in other ways, particularly by cultivating sources. You also don't have free rein to show up at a shareholders meeting or stroll through the office complex, like you can do in public buildings.

Regardless of the challenges, covering business and finance is important and providing a check on powerful industries is a vital part of journalism. So, the old adage in journalism is a truth that still rings true: "follow the money."

Works cited

Wang, S. (2016, April 29). The Wall Street Journal website — paywalled from the very beginning — turns 20 years old today. NiemanLab.

KAREN BLUMENTHAL

Journalist and author

Source: Robin Sachs Photography

My business journalism career nearly ended not long after it began.

As a young Wall Street Journal reporter, I was doing a stint on "spot news," which meant handling the rush of daily news items. The first task of the spot news reporter was to phone in news to the Dow Jones News Service, a real-time financial wire service that provided on-the-spot coverage a gazillion years before the internet.

A complicated, convoluted press release came in about the combination of a bunch of oil partnerships that were being rolled up into one company. I struggled to make sense of the legalese. But because the wire was competitive, I had to call in details of the press release there first, before I could do any reporting to figure it out.

Soon after filing this mess, the company's lawyer called. The New York Stock Exchange had halted trading in the stock until accurate information was on the wire. I had completely botched the news story.

In my mind's eye, I envisioned thousands of traders waiting breathlessly to buy and sell the stock while I slogged back through the press release to undo the damage I'd done.

Luckily, I had a patient and understanding editor, who helped me work through the information and get it straightened out. And, even better, he didn't fire me.

Despite my screw-up, it was this kind of spin and corporate obfuscation that drew me to business journalism in the first place. More than in any other area, financial journalists are crucial to shining light on the workings of big and small businesses, employers, financial firms and product makers who touch every part of our lives.

Almost every other area of hard news that journalists cover has some natural checks and balances. Politicians have opponents and critics, as well as Freedom of Information laws for helping get information about public entities. Courts have natural adversaries. But there are darn few checks on business.

Regulatory agencies? Not really. The Securities and Exchange Commission cares only about corporate disclosure, not bad behavior. There are way, way too many businesses for any consumer-protection agency to truly monitor, and much of the oversight doesn't really help consumers.

Consumer groups? Not enough of them, and they don't have enough funding to really get the word out. As a result, the very people who profit from your credit cards, student and car loans and retirement investments produce the vast amount of financial "education" about those products.

It was the opportunity to offer an independent, well-thought-out perspective that called me to financial journalism. (Plus, in business, just about the worst thing that can happen is that you lose your money. That's bad — but not nearly as heart-wrenching as the murder and tragic destruction that my Metro friends often covered.)

Pro tip

Care deeply, ask lots of questions and become an expert in an area that makes you absolutely indispensable.

It's true that you'll never be wealthy and you'll work a lot of holidays and birthdays and weekends. But here are the main reasons I am — and always will be — a journalist:

- **Yes, it's trite, but journalism really does make a difference.** In financial journalism, you can help steer someone away from a bad financial decision or toward a better one. You can provide information to small investors that keep them from getting run over by the pros. You can call out executives for greedy and self-serving behavior that hurts the little guy.

   There is nothing more powerful than the ability to report and write about something that needs to be said or fixed. That's true whether you're giving readers more information than they currently have, correcting false statements or leveling the playing field between professionals and consumers.

- **Journalists get to act on their righteous indignation.** My husband writes a Wall Street Journal column about travel that is invaluable to road warriors and even periodic vacationers. When he sees an airline or an airport violate its own rules, he gets incensed and wants to fuss. But, I tell him, don't complain. Write about it!

- **You can satisfy your bottomless curiosity — and have access that few other people ever will.** Want to know why your credit score is disappointing? Write about how the system penalizes you far more for missing a payment than for having a lot of debt. Frustrated by all the fees you pay? Expose who is profiting and why.

  Do you need to know why a company is performing poorly or moving into another market? Seek interviews with the executives. Want to know why a product is selling badly or holiday sales are weak? Talk to consumers.

  In my years as a reporter and editor, I had the opportunity to sit down with the top executives of some of the nation's largest companies, as well as out-of-luck people at the unemployment office, government leaders and top thinkers. Your source list is limited only by your imagination and creativity.

- **Journalists have a fair bit of freedom to do their work — even at a young age.** There are very few industries where the rookie's work can get the same play as the veteran's. In journalism, nearly all reporters make their own choices about who to call, what angles to pursue and how to tell a story. Sure, editors may send you back again and again for more detail or they may rewrite your work. But while experienced bosses give directives to young lawyers, young accountants or new business grads, every reporter has a fair bit of personal authority.

  On the web or in print, the bylines look the same. And executives don't know when The Wall Street Journal calls if they are going to talk to a new hire or an old hand. One friend of mine was on his first day as a summer intern when he was assigned a story that required him to interview Donald Trump. (And he did.)

- **We get to research and write for a living, and work with other bright, curious, committed people.** (And you don't have to spend oodles of money on law school!)

  Few people have the opportunity to make a living solely as storytellers. It's a gift to be able to do that, even taking into account the weird hours, modest pay and job insecurities.

  When I started in the journalism business more than 30 years ago, few people stayed past their mid-30s. They worked in journalism for 10 or 15 years and then left for higher-paying pastures. But pay at bigger news organizations has improved quite a bit since then and many of my colleagues put in 30 or more years as reporters and editors.

So how do you make a career of it? Become very good at a specialty that is core to your operation and hard to duplicate. Be the reporter who always has the news first on your beat and who knows more about the industry you cover than some of the people in it. Or the person who has so many sources that she can always find out why an executive was bounced. Or the one who can clearly and insightfully explain what individuals need to know about investing.

Dig deeper. Lots of people know a lot about music or fashion or sports, but not a lot know a lot about the business of music or fashion or sports. Learn how to read financial statements and where to find the documents that deliver insights or details. Those are skills that will benefit you whether you stay in financial journalism or choose another specialty.

One other thing: Consider where the jobs are. When I started in business journalism, many newspapers were just beginning to add daily business sections and were beefing up their staffs. Because it touches so many areas of our daily lives, business and financial journalism has continued to provide above average opportunities to those who are willing to invest in the subject.

Bio

Karen Blumenthal is a veteran financial journalist and the author of 10 books, including three financial books for adults.

A former business editor for The Dallas Morning News, she spent two decades at The Wall Street Journal. There, she covered retailing, oil and gas, housing, mergers and bankruptcies, and was Dallas bureau chief for eight years, supervising a dozen reporters covering an eight-state territory. In that role, she coordinated and edited one of the September 11, 2001 stories that won the 2002 Pulitzer Prize for spot-news reporting.

She has taught business journalism at Texas Christian University and the University of North Texas. In addition to her financial books, she has written seven award-winning nonfiction books for young people.

Career timeline

Author of 10 books, including seven award-winning nonfiction books for young people.

Spring 2016, Reynolds Visiting Business Journalism Professor at the University of North Texas.

2012–2013, business columnist for Texas Monthly magazine.

Spring 2012, Reynolds Visiting Business Journalism Professor at Texas Christian University.

2008–2013, personal finance columnist for The Wall Street Journal.

1994–2006, Dallas deputy bureau chief, Dallas bureau chief and senior editor, Journal Reports for The Wall Street Journal.

1992–1994, business editor for The Dallas Morning News

1990, graduated with an MBA from Southern Methodist University.

1984–1992, reporter and news editor at The Wall Street Journal.

1981–1984, metro and business reporter at The Dallas Morning News.

1981, graduated from Duke University with a bachelor's degree in economics.

KELLI B. GRANT

Personal finance and consumer
reporter, CFP™

CNBC.com

Source: CNBC

Quick — can you tell me what kind of student loans you have? How about where your credit score ranks? Or the total you're paying in fees in your retirement account?

Those would be stumpers for plenty of consumers. What drives me as a journalist is helping people get a better understanding of their finances, so they can use that knowledge to improve their lives.

Financial literacy is a critical skill these days. As consumers, we're being asked to juggle more goals on a limited paycheck. Big ones like buying a home, starting a family, saving for retirement or launching a business. Little ones like taking a vacation, buying a new computer or keeping the fridge full of groceries. Throw mounting student loan debt into the mix — researcher Mark Kantrowitz put the average at $37,172.80 for the Class of 2016 — and it can become a tightrope act.

At the same time, financial products and decisions are increasingly complex. Even opening a credit card requires sifting through dozens of options. A big goal like retirement is practically paralyzing. How much to save? IRA or 401(k) — and what the heck are those, anyway? Which investments are best?

And financial education is all over the map, with many people learning about money primarily from our parents. A Council for Economic Education study found that in 2016, just 17 states require high school students to complete a course in personal finance — the same number that had such a requirement in 2014. The number of states requiring a course in economics dropped from 22 to 20 over the same period.

When people ask me how I got into writing about personal finance they usually assume I have a business background, but I crash-landed into the beat. Growing up, I always wanted to be a journalist. Getting into personal finance journalism was a happy accident.

My love of writing stemmed from an early love of reading. My mom, a teacher at one of the local elementary schools, would sneak me into the library before classes began so I could browse the chapter-book sections that were off-limits to younger grade levels during regular class visits. I'd go home with a backpack full of contraband like "Little House in the Big Woods" and "Bunnicula."

I got my first professional writing gig at age seven, applying through a county library program to write children's book reviews for the Asbury Park Press, one of New Jersey's biggest newspapers. The clip (complete with a headshot of me in all my late-1980s glory — big glasses, bigger hair) is in my portfolio, and two of the books still sit on my bookshelf, waiting for my son to be old enough to read them.

From there, I approached journalism with a single-minded determination, becoming editor for both my middle and high school papers, and contributing to one of the local papers. Ithaca College gave me the opportunity to get hands-on experience immediately. I unpacked my boxes and took on an assignment at the student-run paper, The Ithacan, that same day. By the time I graduated, I was working nearly full-time for two of the regional papers.

Pro tip

Always be networking. You never know when someone you meet will become your next source, mentor or job lead.

But I still had no idea what kind of journalism I wanted to do. Ithaca had classes on magazine journalism, international journalism, long-form storytelling. I took them all. Internships and newsroom experience taught me as much about what I didn't want to do as what I did: I'm a better writer than editor, I prefer the pace of daily newspapers and websites to monthly magazines, and I don't have the right disposition to handle the tough cops and courts beat.

Ithaca Journal editor Bruce Estes was the one who pushed me to follow the money. He sent me to cover the shareholders' meeting of a regional bank, and assigned me enterprise pieces on topics like the economic boost of graduation weekend and the effect new chain stores were having on local businesses.

So when I got an email a month before graduation from an editor at CBS MarketWatch asking me to come in for an interview, I thought, "Why not?"

My resume had ended up in the hands of Marshall Loeb, one of the great names in business journalism. He'd been managing editor of Fortune and Money, as well as the Columbia Journalism Review, and at the time I met him was a senior columnist for CBS MarketWatch. He was looking for a reporter and assistant. My lack of financial knowledge didn't put him off.

He told me that it came back to good journalism: Be a good writer and a smart reporter, and you can learn the beat.

Writing pieces that would have Marshall's name on them was intimidating, to say the least, so I set about learning personal finance any way I could. I wasn't making enough to live in New York City, so I commuted from my parents' house in southern New Jersey. The bus took 95 minutes each way, and I spent that time reading: The Wall Street Journal, "Personal Finance for Dummies" — whatever money books authors had sent to the office hoping for a write-up.

To make sure I had a thorough understanding, I asked sources to explain topics to me as if they were telling someone who'd knew nothing on the subject. I learned right along with my readers, and often tailored pieces to money questions I had. Should I consolidate my student loans? How do I get a great deal on a car? Who do I need to tip at the holidays?

As I learned more about financial journalism, I grew to love the subject matter — and just recently went back to school to get a master's degree in personal financial planning. Marshall and other editors I have worked with taught me to always champion the consumer, to point out where an industry or company was failing them and what they could do to take charge of their financial lives. It's wonderful to know that someone reading my work might come away with some actionable tip or a deeper understanding that helps them avoid a scam, make a smarter spending decision or otherwise improve their finances.

That also boosts the pressure to get it right.

The "personal" in personal finance presents a challenge. What works for me to manage my student loan debt might be different than what works for you, or your cousin across the country — due to differences in location, employer, amount of debt, type of debt, interest rates, marital status, household income and easily a dozen more factors. The story is more about telling people how to weigh their options and find the right solution for themselves, rather than handing them a one-size-fits-all strategy.

Often, we don't know what we don't know. Americans routinely give ourselves high marks in financial literacy surveys — even as we admit to damaging money habits like carrying credit card debt or not having an emergency fund. FINRA's Investor Education Foundation has been asking consumers the same set of five basic money questions for years. In 2009, 42 percent of consumers could answer at least four of the five quiz questions correctly; in 2015, only 37 percent were able to.

Financial literacy isn't one-and-done. It's a constant endeavor, and I'm excited to be part of that education.

Bio

Kelli B. Grant, CFP™, is a writer covering personal finance and consumer spending for CNBC.com. Prior to joining CNBC.com, Grant was the senior consumer reporter for MarketWatch.com and SmartMoney.com. Her work has appeared in The Wall Street Journal, The New York Times, SmartMoney, Kiplinger's Personal Finance, Good Housekeeping, Real Simple and Family Circle, among other publications. She has shared her savings strategies on shows including NBC Nightly News, Today Show, CBS This Morning, CBS Up to the Minute, Inside Edition and Fox & Friends. Grant holds a master's degree in personal financial planning from Kansas State University, and a bachelor's degree in journalism and anthropology from Ithaca College. She is also a certified financial planner. She lives in New Jersey with her husband and their son.

Career timeline

2013–present, personal finance and consumer spending reporter at CNBC. com.

2016, Columbia University fellow, Age Boom Academy.

2016, certified financial planner.

2015, National Press Foundation fellow, Reporting Retirement.

2011, Best in Business Award, Society for American Business Editors and Writers.

2007–2013, senior consumer reporter at SmartMoney.com/MarketWatch. com. (SmartMoney.com folded into MarketWatch.com in 2011, when SmartMoney magazine closed.)

2005–2007, consumer reporter for SmartMoney.com.

2004–2005, reporter and assistant to Marshall Loeb at CBS MarketWatch.

MICHAEL SCHREIBER

Founder

Amalgamated Unlimited

Some journalists wind up in in this business very purposefully. They know what they want to do, and they remain laser-focused on getting there no matter what obstacles confront them. Investigative journalists are often like this. It's almost a compulsion. Others ... how to put this? ... are more opportunistic. They pursue journalism, because it interests them at the time. They work one beat, and then they tire of it, so the get on another, and then they tire of that, so they move from print to digital, and then to TV. As opportunities come their way, they pursue them, because they find them to be interesting ... well, more interesting than the last thing they were covering, anyway.

There's no shame in being an opportunistic journalist. I should know. I am one.

The route I took from being City Hall reporter on a small daily paper, to eventually running a financial news site was circuitous. Here's the quick version of the story.

I got my first job at a small daily in upstate New York. I covered City Hall and wrote two or three stories a day. It was excellent training. From there I headed south to New York City, where after working a series of non-journalism jobs and doing some traveling, I enrolled in the Columbia Graduate School of Journalism to learn how to make TV. Then I worked in a few different long form video outfits, including ABC News, HBO, The New York Times and "Frontline." While I was at the Times I helped produce an episode of "Frontline" called "The Secret

History of the Credit Card." The producer/correspondent was Lowell Bergman and the film was essentially a hidden-in-plain-sight investigation into how credit cards actually work. It was one of the first documentaries ever to feature Elizabeth Warren, now a U.S. senator.

No one thought much of that idea initially because the footage was going to be so bland (credit cards?). We were wrong. Creative storytelling on the part of my bosses combined with the fact that, while everyone has credit cards no one knows how they work made for a very compelling documentary. It won a ton of awards, including a DuPont and an Emmy.

Shortly thereafter, New York Times Television, which produced that and other Frontline pieces I worked on, closed down. I bounced around a bit. I worked on more documentaries. I worked at a startup. I did an episode of Wife Swap. Then, largely because of my experience on the credit card documentary, I landed at Jim Cramer's financial news site TheStreet.com. I became managing editor of the personal finance site MainStreet.com, and it was there where I learned the intricacies of online news and syndication. After a couple of years at TheStreet, I was hired by Credit.com.

Pro tip

Use your reporting skills to learn the business fundamentals of journalism! Some questions to ponder: Is your company profitable? Why or why not? If you were to build your own news site, what revenue model would you employ? Journalism is at a critical juncture: we need good journalists more than ever, but collectively we're having trouble paying for good journalism. It's up to each of us to help solve this problem.

Credit.com was among the first websites to offer users a free credit score. They had a roster of experts and contributors who wrote articles about credit, but I was brought on to reshape the "content" team into a more traditional news team. The goal wasn't just to develop an audience on Credit.com, but more importantly to syndicate our articles to other news sites. Generally speaking, syndication relationships can help sites grow traffic in a variety of ways: through linking, SEO and general awareness. That's why so many sites syndicate and share content among themselves.

Any site that wants to develop news syndication relationships must develop and implement all the standards and practices of a "traditional" news organization. Beyond that, however, is the fact that this strategy is essentially a new kind of business model for online journalism.

Traditionally, online news has employed a CPM ad model (CPM stands for cost per mille). Banner ads surround content, and for every 1,000 ad impressions, the publisher is paid a certain amount. This model incentivizes the publisher to get as many ad impressions as possible, which usually means more pageviews. Since readers typically consume news over a finite period of time, publishers have to push as many ads and pageviews as possible. That's why there's so much click-bait out there. Click-bait, however, isn't terribly engaging. People check it out, they may quickly click through a number of pages, or slides, and then they typically bounce. They usually don't hang out long enough on the page to see the ads, much less absorb and click on them. The advertisers know this because they can tell that people aren't clicking on the ads (that's the big difference between online and print ads — no one knows just how many eyeballs that ad on page 15 actually got). All of this has driven the price of these ads down, which means that the publishers must get even more pageviews to make the same amount of money. It's a vicious circle, and is a big reason why the news business is in so much trouble these days.

Financial sites often don't rely on a CPM model, however. They may employ a CPA model. CPA stands for cost per acquisition. Financial sites are basically a form of e-commerce. When someone shops for a credit card or any other financial product, and they ultimately purchase it, the site is likely paid what amounts to a finder's fee. That means that the sites are incentivized to match people with products for which they are likely to qualify, but more importantly, it means that the sites must foster a relationship with their readers built on trust and credibility. Readers need to feel that they can trust the news and information on these sites or they certainly can't be expected to buy anything. Plus, since mere pageviews are no longer the goal, reporters and editors are incentivized to create truly engaging content that provides information that readers actually need.

Media companies big and small are beginning to explore how to incorporate e-commerce into their operations. In October 2016, The New York Times announced that it had purchased the consumer review site The Wirecutter for more than $30 million. What makes The Wirecutter unique among New York Times properties is that its revenue model is based on e-commerce. They'll write about a product, but somewhere within that article there will be a "buy" that will direct the reader to a site like Amazon (with which The Wirecutter has an affiliate relationship) and if the reader indeed buys the item, The Wirecutter will get paid some percentage of the purchase price.

In order for this, or any new model to work, the foundational principles of journalism must be in place. Transparency is key. Readers should understand the nature of the advertising model, and reporters and editors — as well as corporate leadership — must respect and observe the traditional line in the sand between sales and editorial. Journalism through all its iterations has been replete with appearances of conflicts of interest. Media organizations frequently report on companies that advertise with them. In some cases, media organizations are owned by companies they report on. This e-commerce model is really no different in my opinion. Reporters and editors must be able to cover everyone — positively and negatively — regardless of whether they advertise on the site; CPA and CPM ads alike. I anticipate more and more companies will begin getting into journalism and hiring people like us to do the work. It will be up to us to make sure they understand where the lines in the sand are, and what is and isn't permissible. Those conversations aren't always easy, but they are vital.

I spend a lot of time thinking about the business of journalism these days. I think about the craft too, but I'm pretty preoccupied with the business. It's not how I imagined things would go for me when I began my career, but I'm far from the only one thinking about these issues. These days, understanding the business of journalism is really a necessity for anyone in the field. More of us will have to go it alone at some point in our careers but luckily individual journalists have never had more tools at their disposal to connect directly with audiences. We just can't afford to be blind to the business fundamentals that make our work possible. In addition to protecting democracy, we've all got to eat, after all.

Bio

Michael Schreiber is the founder of Amalgamated Unlimited, a company devoted to creating new ways to connect creators (including journalists) with the companies that need them. Previously he was editor-in-chief and chief content officer at Credit.com. He's worked at The New York Times, "Frontline," ABC News, TheStreet.com, HBO and was an adjunct professor at the Graduate School of Journalism at Columbia University (a school he attended with Aaron Chimbel, the editor of this book). He has a bachelor's degree in psychology from Skidmore College.

Career timeline

2017–present, founder of Amalgamated Unlimited.
2010–2017, editor-in-chief and chief content officer at Credit.com.
2009–2010, managing editor of TheStreet.com's personal finance website, MainStreet.com.
2006–2008, director of operations at TV360.
2004–2005, associate producer for The New York Times/Frontline.
2003–2005/2005–2006, associate producer at ABC News.
1998–1999, reporter at The Saratogian in New York.

Sports journalists

For a lot of people, covering sports seems like the best job possible. After all, you get paid to attend games, go to practices and interview athletes. There are certainly many worse ways to make a living than to be a sports journalist.

But, and there is a big one, for many sports journalists the job changes how you experience sports. It's not all fun and games.

For starters, there are some important ground rules for covering sports: there is no cheering in the press box and no asking for autographs. You are there to do a job. You are no longer a fan when you cover a team or sport, just as it would be unacceptable for a political reporter to be cheering for a candidate.

Good sports journalism goes beyond what happens on a field or court, in a pool or on the course because sports are a major part of our society and the implications of sports are profound.

Athletes are often activists and their actions become part of a national dialogue that can bring attention to issues in a way few others can. We've seen this in Colin Kaepernick's National Anthem protest about treatment of people of color in the United States, and other athletes have spoken out about domestic violence, and teams and leagues promote breast cancer awareness and other causes.

Sports intersect with politics in terms of public financing of stadiums and Olympic bids, while also connecting communities via civic pride.

Unfortunately, many sports journalists are required to cover the crimes of athletes and issues of domestic and sexual violence.

As a sports journalist, you are usually working when games are going, meaning nights and weekends, which can be difficult to maintain work–life balance.

Like much of journalism, the job outlook for sports journalists has been mixed in recent years, with newspapers and local television stations cutting sports staffs, while at the same time many niche websites cover all manner of sports and a slew of new cable stations have hours to fill.

Because sport is so central to our society, the demand for information about the teams and athletes we follow is insatiable and that's good news for people who want to cover sports.

KAREN CROUSE

Sportswriter

The New York Times

Source: The New York Times

I am a journalist because of a man who, as a 19 year old, altered the course of my life — and his — with a simple act of generosity. It was 1976 and I was living in California and nearing the end of eighth grade. My English teacher assigned a project: create a magazine. I was a competitive swimmer, so mine was called Splash, to be anchored by a Q&A with a swimmer. But which one?

To my father, a salesman with a gift for persuasion, the answer was obvious: Mike Bruner. Bruner, the best swimmer on my club team, was also one of the top performers in the world. He was 19, a mechanical engineering major at Stanford who was favored to make the 1976 United States squad in multiple events. He had a shaved head and might as well have had winged feet given his exalted status among my peer group.

I was so shy, I couldn't summon the courage to talk to the cute boy who sat next to me at school. How was I going to manage a conversation with this chlorine king? I told my father there was no way I would be able to interview Bruner. No. Way. The next day, with my father at my side lest I lose my nerve, I approached the head coach, Bill Rose, who had worked with Bruner for several years, and haltingly explained my project. Rose listened attentively, and when I was through he said, "Have your questions ready tomorrow, and I'll make sure Mike speaks to you."

Years later, I found out that Rose told Bruner to stay after practice for an interview. Bruner, not unreasonably, assumed the request had come from a reporter from The San Jose Mercury-News, Sports Illustrated or some other news media outlet. Imagine his surprise when he was greeted by a pigtailed pipsqueak holding 3-by-5 notecards in her trembling hands. If Bruner was disappointed, he didn't show it. He graciously answered all my questions.

After the project was graded, I made two extra copies of Splash for Rose and Bruner. I was so excited for them to see that I had received an A for my efforts (and theirs). As it happened, shortly thereafter I attended the Olympic trials in Long Beach, Calif., with my father, who arranged the trip as my graduation gift. The night before we arrived, Bruner failed to make the Olympic team in the 400m freestyle. Earlier, he was fourth in the 200 freestyle, missing the team by one spot, although he qualified for the 800 freestyle relay.

Bruner, disappointed at the way his meet was unfolding, was not in a positive frame of mind for his best event, the 200 butterfly, on the day we arrived. I was able to reach the pool deck and deliver my magazine to Rose, who leafed through it. After reading the Q&A with Bruner, he said: "This is great! Mike needs to read this right now."

Off he went in search of Bruner, who was having "a pity party," Rose said. He found Bruner underneath the stands, in a foul mood as he went through the motions of preparing for the 200 butterfly preliminaries. Rose said he shoved the Q&A in Bruner's face and made him read his answers out loud.

Pro tip

Unplug from your devices and open your eyes and ears to what is happening right under your nose.

He made him repeat this response to a question on the role of mental attitude in racing: "I'd say that swimming is at least 90 percent mental. You can work harder than anyone but lose a race because you don't have a positive attitude. The swimmer with the best attitude is the one that will win the race."

Bruner, in effect, delivered his own pep talk. He went out and made the Olympic team in the 200 butterfly. When he met with reporters after the final, he was asked how he overcame the disappointments of his earlier races to swim so well. This is what he said: "A little girl from the club interviewed me for a class project and had gotten an A on the paper. In it, I talked a lot about hard work, having the will to win and things like that. Reading it brought me back to reality. I think I gave up in the 400 free."

Bruner's quotation appeared in a sports article in The Long Beach Press-Telegram the next day. Rose produced a copy for me. The older swimmers on the team made a fuss, treating me as if I had just made my first Olympic team. I read and reread the line. It was hard for me to imagine that something I had written could have helped somebody, much less our club's chlorine king, realize his Olympic dream. Bruner went on to win Olympic gold medals in the 200 butterfly and the 800 freestyle relay at the 1976 Summer Olympics in Montreal.

Knowing that I had played a part in Bruner's success was an indescribable feeling. For someone who was afraid of her shadow, it was empowering to realize that I not only had a voice, it was powerful enough to move mountains. I remember turning to my father on the pool deck and saying: "This is what I want to do when I grow up. I want to write about people and positively affect their lives." So that is the long story of how I became a journalist: because a teenager who was kind of a big deal took a few minutes out of his day to talk to me, and through that conversation, a whole new world indirectly opened up to me.

I wasn't drawn to the business by fame or fortune. I didn't care how much (or how little) journalists were paid. My goal was never to win a Pulitzer, work at a major paper, become a television personality or change the world. I was motivated by the simple desire to tell people's stories and positively impact people's lives. That is the meat and potatoes of my professional existence. Everything else is the gravy.

As time went on, I realized my reasons for becoming a journalist were more complicated. All those stories I thought I was writing to shine a light on other people's lives, I was really doing to make better sense of my own. Over the years, it has also dawned on me that I became a journalist for the same reason that many people probably become actors: my press badge allowed me to inhabit worlds that otherwise would have been off-limits to me. It has afforded me access to interesting people that I otherwise might never meet. As a child, I read stories to learn about people and places. As an adult, I learn about people and places by writing stories. Journalism has brought my life full circle.

Bio

Karen Crouse grew up in northern California and is a graduate of St. Francis High School in Mountain View and the University of Southern California, where she majored in journalism and minored in chlorine as a member of the women's swim team. She has been at The New York Times for 10 years, the last five as the golf writer. In 2016, she covered the Olympics in Rio de Janeiro, her 10th Olympics, where she wrote about Michael Phelps, Katie Ledecky and the 74-year-old woman who coached the runner who won the 400m in world record time.

Career timeline

The New York Times is her ninth newspaper job.

Her first job was at Swimming World magazine out of college.

Two of the papers she worked for no longer exist; one (the Los Angeles Herald-Examiner) stopped publishing in 1989 while she was working there.

MARK GODICH

Senior editor

Sports Illustrated

As early as the seventh grade, I had it in my mind that I was going to be a sportswriter. I fancied myself as having a way with words, and when I wasn't riding the bench as the third-string quarterback at Richardson West Junior High in suburban Dallas, I spent a fair amount of time writing about the Broncos for The West Wind, the student newspaper. My football career ended not long after, but my passion for writing only intensified. I moved on to be the sports editor of the Talon at Richardson High School and freelanced for the local paper. I studied journalism at the University of Missouri — the only school to which I applied — and my first job out of school was in the sports department of the Reporter-News in sleepy Abilene, Texas.

No doubt about it: I was on my way as a sportswriter.

Then came the rude awakening. As I was exploring my next career move, an executive high on the masthead at the Dallas Times Herald said he saw me as a pedestrian writer. Talk about a kick in the gut. I respected his opinion, however, and he was quick to add that he believed I had a future in the business as an editor. He had heard good things about my work ethic, my management skills, my ability to communicate. Perhaps sensing my disappointment — doesn't every journalist want to be a writer? — he mentioned that editors were typically on a faster track to the top because they were in the office regularly and could witness and better understand what was required to publish a daily newspaper. And that is the day I truly became a journalist.

Why do I do it? Why the fascination? It's simple. I relish the opportunity to come up with a plan, to report, to interpret, to analyze, to help tell a story. I enjoy collaborating with the writer, picking his or her brain for ideas, suggesting revises and making edits while treating the copy as if it were my own. I embrace the challenge of meeting firm and fast deadlines; in fact, it gives me an adrenalin rush. I love to fight for cover stories and advocate on behalf of my writers, trying to convince the boss that a profile that had been budgeted for four pages deserves maybe double the space. I get excited as a project comes together: working with photographers, photo editors, fact-checkers and graphic designers, among others; matching the words with the images; writing a headline and captions that might persuade a reluctant reader to dive in. It takes a village.

Over the years I have been blessed to experience this rush across a wide range of journalistic entities. Dallas was in the midst of a heated newspaper war when I worked at the Times Herald, and the battle between the sports departments was especially intense. The Associated Press was (and remains) a deadline-every-minute operation. The National Sports Daily was cutting-edge, a venture that sadly was slightly ahead of its time. And I have watched Sports Illustrated evolve from a single product with a weekly deadline into an entity with multiple platforms that runs 24/7 — a magazine on crack cocaine, as one former colleague described it.

Pro tip

Great writing starts with exhaustive reporting and research. If you're struggling to put words on your computer screen, chances are you don't have everything you need to construct your story. If time allows, don't be afraid to go back to sources with more questions. And when you are ready to write, consider organizing your thoughts with a rough outline. You'll be amazed at how easily the words will flow.

You don't get into this business for the money, and if you're looking to punch the clock in a nine-to-five routine, don't even think about it. Don't care for toiling on nights and weekends? This isn't for you. But what makes this line of work so intriguing and exhilarating is that ever-looming news development, the awareness that a mundane Monday can turn manic in an instant. The reward comes in showing an ability to react to the news, to find the story inside the story.

What makes a good journalist? Throw the word out there, and for most people the first word that comes to mind is writer. Yet while I envy the ability of colleagues to produce flowing prose, often under ridiculous deadline pressure, for my money I'll take a solid writer who knows how to report. In fact, the best writers are exceptional at their craft because they are reporters first. On the rare occasion a story is kicked back or killed, the most likely reason is because it's been poorly reported. We work in an information business, and those who complain about writer's block probably haven't done the reporting necessary to turn a concept into a story. I still refer to a letter I received after my senior year of high school from a graduate of the Missouri School of Journalism. Of the school's rigorous curriculum, he wrote: "Of those 35 hours of straight journalism you are permitted to take, almost all will stress reporting, laying out advertising, reporting, writing magazine articles, reporting, setting type, reporting, editing copy, reporting, reviewing (not criticizing) books, reporting and more reporting." You get the point.

We are all reporters — the writer, the editor who picks up something on TV or in a newspaper clip, the photographer who sees an exchange between a player and a coach, the fact-checker who uncovers a nugget during research or passes along an idea to a more accomplished writer. Some of SI's best work has started with one idea in mind, only to go in an entirely different direction. It's all in the reporting.

One of the things I have come to appreciate most about this business is the opportunity to reinvent oneself, and it was my passion for reporting that inspired me to write a book that was published in 2013. I felt I had gotten a bit stale in my job, and I was looking for a challenge. Nevertheless, after having written nothing more than the occasional short piece over the previous 25 years, I found the prospect of generating 100,000 words daunting. But I believed I could pull it off if I was willing to report, report, report.

It helped that I was equally passionate about college football. One of the beauties of sports journalism is that you can be a journalist and a fan; you just have to know when to draw the line. Many of us in the sports media are frustrated athletes who, because of our deficiencies, are fascinated with elite players, coaches and other sports figures and want to better understand what makes them tick.

Even as I dug deep into my research and reporting on the book, the work never felt like a chore. Interviews became conversations. Sources made unsolicited calls to provide more details. I gained a new appreciation for players and coaches and a better understanding of the intricacies of the game. The writing, however pedestrian it occasionally seems, came easily. I'm certain that was because I left no stone unturned, reported to no end. The project became a labor of love. It reminded me why I had wanted to be a journalist.

And it confirmed, once and for all, that the curious kid reporter had made the right decision.

Bio

After graduating from the University of Missouri School of Journalism in 1979, Mark Godich landed his first job, as a sportswriter and copy editor at the Reporter-News in Abilene, Texas.

He returned to his alma mater in the summer of 1982 as an instructor in the journalism school and the sports editor of the Columbia Missourian.

At the Dallas Times Herald (February 1984 to October 1988), he worked on the sports desk and as an assistant editor before being promoted to executive sports editor. His tenure came during a time when the award-winning staff uncovered rules and recruiting violations in Southwest Conference football programs, including SMU, which was handed the death penalty by the NCAA. After a year at the Associated Press, Godich was hired as a senior editor in charge of college basketball and golf coverage at The National Sports Daily in New York City; however, the startup publication lasted only 17 months. He then ventured into magazines as the managing editor and then executive editor at Golf Shop Operations, the trade magazine for Golf Digest.

Since 1995, he has been a senior editor at Sports Illustrated, overseeing the magazine's NFL, college football, horse racing and golf beats at various times. He is also the author of "Tigers vs. Jayhawks: From the Civil War to the Battle for No. 1." The book dissects the 2007 football game between Missouri and Kansas, bitter rivals who went from unranked at the start of the season to playing for the top ranking in the country on the Saturday after Thanksgiving.

Career timeline

June 1995–present, senior editor, Sports Illustrated.

2016, panelist for and contributor to the Sports Illustrated book, "College Football's Greatest."

2013, author of the college football book, "Tigers vs. Jayhawks: From the Civil War to the Battle for No. 1."

2012, panelist for and contributor to the Sports Illustrated book, "Football's Greatest."

1991–1995, managing editor; executive editor of Golf Shop Operations (trade publication for Golf Digest).

1989–1991, senior editor at The National Sports Daily.

1988–1989, newsman for Associated Press.

1984–1988, sports copy editor; deputy sports editor; executive sports editor at the Dallas Times Herald.

1982–1984, instructor and sports editor of the Columbia Missourian, University of Missouri School of Journalism.

1979–1982, sportswriter, Abilene Reporter-News.

May 1979, Graduated from the University of Missouri-Columbia with a Bachelor of Journalism degree.

JOEL ANDERSON

Senior national writer

BuzzFeed News

I had been talking to James Curtis Hicks, a 53-year-old grandfather and disabled former truck driver, for about an hour when he warned me that he was getting emotional. He removed the black-rimmed glasses from his fleshy face, struggled to his feet, and grabbed a box of tissues off the kitchen counter. His eyes were red and teary.

We had spent the previous hour in his neat little living room in South Georgia charting the course of his life almost up to that very moment, when he was facing felony voter fraud charges that carried a five-year prison sentence.

"It's saddening to me," he told me. He plopped back down in his chair.

As a child, Mr. Hicks bounced between his father's home in New Orleans and his mother's in Douglas, Georgia, a dusty town of 12,000 between Atlanta and Jacksonville. As a teenager, he gravitated toward the small-town life and its restless streets. As a middle-aged man, he left those streets — and, inevitably, prison — behind for a more stable life as a father and long-haul trucker. He built a life that he was proud of.

After a bad accident left him unable to work in 2011, Mr. Hicks became something of a community leader and had started leading voter-registration drives. In 2012, he backed a candidate who surprised many by defeating the incumbent county sheriff. In March 2016, Mr. Hicks got a letter from the Georgia Secretary of State's Office alleging that he provided too much help to voters and had broken the law.

That's what had brought me all the way from Palo Alto, California, to his tidy doublewide in Douglas, only a few weeks before Election Day. No one had told his story before and he was eager to have it told, even as he — formerly gregarious and almost bubbly — failed to conceal his grief.

"You sit here, bust your butt, pay your debt to society, get your life in order thinking when you're doing the right thing. And then they shoot you down. What have we done to people so bad that they just hate to see black people get ahead in life, have a voice in their community?"

Mr. Hicks' question hung in the air, our first real pause of the afternoon. He wiped his eyes, and we moved on.

On the trip back to my hotel room, on the flight back to California, and at the desk at my home writing this essay, that moment kept returning to me. Not because I had an answer, but because it is this very question — although I had never articulated it quite that way — that has been a guidepost for my journalism career.

The path started just outside Houston, where I was raised by parents — both of whom would've been professional writers themselves in a better and fairer time — who described a world to me that I could scarcely recognize through a child's eyes. They were raised in Arkansas and Louisiana in the 1950s and 1960s.

My father recalled being chased home by a pickup truck full of white teenagers who screamed "nigger" at him. My mother told me of a time when her father — my stoic grandfather who raised 12 children with only a fourth-grade education — left work in tears because a white supervisor had kicked him flush in the ass. And those were just some of the personal indignities, not those writ large like the segregated neighborhoods, schools, and water fountains that typified the Jim Crow South.

As a child, so much of this seemed inexplicable to me. And because it was inexplicable, I wondered if my parents had taken liberties with their memories. By comparison, my life wasn't nearly so melodramatic: I went to integrated schools and I had white friends. I certainly had no fear of racist violence. I was free to concern myself with more frivolous things, like someday playing in the NFL.

By the time I arrived at college at TCU in Fort Worth, Texas, it was obvious the only way I would get into the NFL was as a reporter. So, once I realized my stint on TCU's scout team would likely be indefinite, I presented myself before the editorial staff of the college newspaper: they made me cover the football team. I interviewed my old teammates and excavated details about their lives away from the field I might have never discovered otherwise: one had been homeless as a child, one had spent a month in juvenile detention, and another had released a gospel album with his twin brother. I didn't ask them much about football.

Pro tip

It's best to approach every story or assignment as if your assumptions are wrong or very poorly informed. They probably are, anyway. But pursuing a story from that vantage point makes it much more likely that you won't lean on incorrect assumptions or previously reported material that relied upon its own incorrect assumptions. You might even learn or reveal something new.

I covered less football after college. I also moved around a lot — to Shreveport, to Oklahoma City, back to Houston, Atlanta, Tampa, New York, Washington, D.C. — and began wondering why the obstacles and frustrations felt so similar (red or blue, right or left, Republican or Democratic, homogenous or diverse) in such dissimilar places. The areas with the fewest resources had the least access to the services they needed most. Organizers were devising ways to best press for equity and equality in places that had neither. No one anywhere had reached any sort of peace with their local law enforcement agencies. I found this to be true whether my assignments took me to Staten Island, Seattle or South Georgia.

I might have concluded that the fault for this bleak state of affairs — in almost every corner of our country, even — belonged largely with people whom resembled my parents, my uncles and aunts, my friends, even Mr. Hicks. But there seemed to be something more there. These conditions had the unmistakable echoes of the stories my parents tried to pass on to me as a child.

What strange relief it was then to learn in recent years that the Department of Justice discovered that the Ferguson, Mo. police had engaged in a "pattern and practice of unconstitutional police conduct" against black residents. Federal investigators found the same patterns and practices in the police departments of Baltimore and San Francisco. In North Carolina, a federal appeals court discovered the state's strict voter ID law had largely "targeted" black voters. A recent report by ProPublica found that black children across the South "now attend majority-black schools at levels not seen in four decades" and that "the achievement gap between black and white students, which greatly narrowed during the era in which schools grew more integrated, widened as they became less so."

In the weeks before Election Day, it wasn't lost on me and many others that the nation seemed poised — and nearly unbothered about it — to elect a real estate magnate who had settled a housing discrimination lawsuit in the 1970s.

That's a large part of what drew me to Douglas, Ga., and the story of Mr. Hicks. I wanted to know more about why our country seemed bound for a future that looked an awful lot like my parents' past. What have we done to people so bad?

Far from being paralyzed by his grief, Mr. Hicks said he felt emboldened by what he felt were broad efforts to shut down his work and silence his voice in the community. "It makes me want to change it that much more," he told me. "It makes me want to get this thing right."

It's never been more clear why I'm a journalist. At the very least, I owe my parents and Mr. Hicks and many others my vigilance in asserting our stories and our humanity and our place in this country.

I owe them an answer to their question.

Bio

Joel Anderson is a senior national writer at BuzzFeed News. He writes news and narrative stories about the role of race, justice, and sports in American life — from reporting from the streets of Ferguson and Baltimore during protests, to profiling professional athletes and public figures. In his 15-year career he's worked at the Associated Press, the Tampa Bay Times, the Atlanta Journal-Constitution, and the Shreveport Times, covering beats including cops, courts, city hall, and sports from the high school to professional levels. He's been a contributor to ESPN The Magazine. His 2014 piece, "The Two Michael Sams," is featured in The Best American Sportswriting 2015.

Career timeline

2015–present, senior national writer, BuzzFeed News.
2013–2015, senior sports reporter, BuzzFeed News.
2012–2013, sports reporter, Tampa Bay Times.
2010–2012, reporter, Atlanta Journal-Constitution.
2007–2010, reporter, St. Petersburg Times.
2006–2007, reporter, Shreveport Times.
2004–2005, sports writer, Associated Press—Houston.
2003–2004, sports writer/editor, Associated Press—Oklahoma City.
2001–2003, newsman (yes, it was really called that), Associated Press—Dallas.

Print journalists

There's no way around it: These are tough times for newspapers and magazines. Printed news is and has been for several years in crisis mode in the wake of a drastic drop in advertising revenue.

Even with that grim summary, newspapers continue to do indispensable work and the journalists who work there are vital to the communities they serve.

While major newspapers like The New York Times, USA Today, The Washington Post and The Wall Street Journal get the most attention, and certainly do a lot of important work on national and international issues, it is local newspapers that are the main check on those in power in counties, cities and towns across the country. Without those papers covering school boards and county commissioner's courts and state agencies, elected officials and bureaucrats may be unencumbered to do whatever they wish, and out of view of the public they are designated to serve.

Certainly, local broadcast stations and the new breed of digital news organizations, many of them nonprofits, provide some of that coverage, but historically it has been local newspapers that have driven such reporting. The breadth of what newspapers have traditionally done is hard to replicate and was funded by a business model that worked because of limited competition and a broad reach that served advertisers well. Now, advertisers have fled to cheaper and more targeted digital alternatives and the once fat classified sections have become victim to Craigslist, Monster and other engaging online options. In turn, newspapers have lost more than $30 billion in advertising revenue over the past decade.

That's the bad news, and there is considerable bad news, but there is also a lot to be excited about as print outlets dive deeper into becoming digital news organizations that happen to publish a printed product. The journalism produced by newspapers is, generally, some of the best anywhere and digital innovations connect that work with much wider audiences than was ever possible before.

Change is hard and newspapers and magazines are in the midst of great change, and have been for more than a decade now and will likely be for many years to come. However, the work truly changes lives and the world and the platform of a newspaper is still very powerful.

Works cited

Lichterman, J. (2015, April 29). The State of the News Media 2015: Newspapers ↓, smart-phones ↑. NiemanLab.

TAWNELL D. HOBBS

National education reporter

The Wall Street Journal

As a journalist, I'm the messenger. My job is to tell the public what they need to know and won't hear from governmental officials. I highlight the shortcomings of those who seek to misuse taxpayers' money, while bringing attention to important issues that impact communities.

The job of a journalist isn't easy but is necessary in a civil society. Today's newspaper reporter is faced with financial struggles in the business, leading to downsized newsrooms and operations. Those who choose to stay are challenged with heavier workloads during a time of increased skepticism of the news media, exacerbated by a growth of fake news stories on social media.

But a need to inform the public is why I remain a journalist. I'm a longtime education reporter, which I consider one of the best beats in the business. Covering education extends beyond the classroom, and touches on politics, finances, crime, courts and civil rights.

I have been able to shine a light on a series of issues — from a story that revealed millions in frivolous spending in a public school district to one that exposed a weak background-check system that allowed felons unfettered access to classrooms.

Being a reporter extends beyond interviewing and writing, it involves an ability to be neutral, flexible, calm and fair — even in situations that seem the most unfair.

I remember tagging along with police officers doing checks on sex offenders by visiting their homes. At one home, a grandfatherly man answered the door.

I came to find out that he had been convicted of molesting children. He consented to an interview, and I sat in his home and listened to him tell me how he gained access to his victims by babysitting them. It's a memory that I will never forget. I remained neutral throughout the interview. My job requires me to tamp down personal feelings.

Journalists are not judge and jury. And even when the jury renders its decision, we still have to be neutral. Every story must be entered with an open mind. There is no black, white or brown in reporting. There are no religious or political affiliations.

Not to say that journalists should overlook bad judgment and discrepancies. But we have to stick to the facts and believe that readers are smart enough to use them to make up their minds.

Journalism is a good fit for me because I'm curious by nature, and I like to write and learn about new things. Newsgathering is an educational process, opening the mind to unknown facts and unfamiliar topics. I haven't worked on too many stories without learning something new. This is a field where you don't have to be a know-it-all — but one where you should feel comfortable asking questions, even the difficult ones. If you don't have an inquiring mind, journalism is not for you.

Pro tip

Always do the job of a journalist with integrity, fairness and accuracy.

I'm always ready to step outside my comfort zone, which has helped in my journalism career. Stories that take me out of my norm — such as the time this education reporter covered a hot-air balloon crash — are the ones I relish because they challenge me and I'm bound to learn something new.

Being a journalist has allowed me to step into places that I never dreamed of going, such as the time I covered floods in Louisiana, or visited the hometown of a serial killer for a profile, or sat with Arnold Schwarzenegger to talk about a program he sponsored for underprivileged children.

The job can be fast-paced. Reporters have to always be ready to shift gears. Not too many days are the same, or at least they shouldn't be as the world is constantly changing. As a journalist, I watch for those changes and look for trends that connect people. My passion to get to the bottom of a story drives me.

I like bringing the news to the public and letting them know what they should be thinking about and why. With every story, a journalist should be able to answer the "why." Why is this important? Why should the public care? If you can't answer those questions, than you shouldn't be doing the story.

My job comes with great responsibility, and therefore some stress. What I write can have lasting impact. Imagine thousands or even millions of people reading a story that has the power to shape opinions and influence decisions.

With so much at stake, stories have to be fair, accurate and balanced. These principles apply even in an era of fast news and the desire to be first to publish a story. It should be noted that a news organization that gets a big story wrong will be remembered more than the one that was first to publish by a few minutes.

As a journalist, being able to empathize is a must as we are sometimes thrust into emotional situations. Imagine being sent to interview the mother who just lost a son in Iraq or a family whose home was destroyed in a tornado, both situations I have dealt with. The last thing you want to be is a pushy reporter. If the family doesn't want to talk, ask if there is a family spokesperson who might. If nothing else, leave your business card in case they feel up to talking later. They will remember the reporter who showed respect.

Being a reporter doesn't end at the end of a shift. You just don't turn it off. It stays with you, whether on social media, at a public event or online. There are things you cannot do, such as erecting a campaign sign in your yard or taking to Twitter to tell the board president on your beat that his idea is silly. And going out and getting arrested will probably get you prominent mention by the local media. Maintaining a good reputation is important, without it you will lose your credibility.

The job includes being entrusted with information and insight not easily accessible to the public. It's along that vein that I warn of the influence that comes with the position. People will want to be associated with you. They will offer you gifts. They will want to wine and dine you, be in your circle. Please resist.

I'm not saying that you can't have lunch with someone on your beat (by the way, always pay or go Dutch), but the relationship should always be professional. Don't blur the lines. And as a beat reporter for many years, I will tell you that the ability to balance these relationships is an art — and it isn't always easy. The people that you cover on a beat are the same ones you rely on for information, necessitating some kind of relationship.

Some people you meet in your reporting career will gain the title of "source," these are your go-to people that will provide tips and take you behind the scenes. The ability to cultivate sources is a must for a journalist. Please know that the best news stories don't come laid out in a tidy package by a public relations office.

I've always said that journalism is not a job for those who have a need to be liked by everyone. If that is your desire, you're in the wrong field. News stories can bring negative feedback and backlash — but they also can bring thanks and praise from an informed public.

And that is why I'm a journalist.

Bio

Tawnell Hobbs is the national K–12 education reporter for The Wall Street Journal. She has worked at the Journal since July 2016, and before that was an education reporter at The Dallas Morning News for 16 years. Hobbs also was a reporter at the Fort Worth Star-Telegram, covering a bevy of topics. She has won numerous local, state and national awards. Most recently in 2016, Hobbs was part of a team that won a National Headliner Award for education writing.

Before starting her journalism career, Hobbs served in the United States Air Force and the Texas Air National Guard, for a combined total of about 10 years. She has also taught computer-assisted reporting at the university level.

Career timeline

2016–present, national K–12 education reporter at The Wall Street Journal.
2000–2016, education reporter The Dallas Morning News.
2008–2015, adjunct professor at Texas Christian University teaching computer-assisted information gathering.
1998–2000, reporter at the Fort Worth Star Telegram.
1993–1998, Texas Air National Guard, enlisted.
1989–1993, United States Air Force, enlisted.

ROSE BACA

Staff photographer

The Dallas Morning News

It's the question I get asked the most when I'm working. What's the coolest photo you've ever taken? I know what they're expecting. They want to hear about a hot air balloon ride, or what it's like to photograph a Dallas Cowboys game. But for the life of me, when I'm asked, my mind always, without fail, goes blank. I can't think of one single "cool" story to tell them. It's pretty disappointing to watch me struggle. It's made me think a lot about my lack of ability to simply just answer the question, and why nothing ever so easily comes to mind. I've been taking photos for The Dallas Morning News since early 2010. I've gone on a lot of assignments. The hot air balloon ride? Yeah, it was amazing in the whimsical sense that for once in my life I was literally moving wherever the wind took me. And there's really nothing like photographing an NFL game on the sidelines. But these experiences are not the first thing on my mind. It's the people.

In many ways journalism completely changed my personality. How I view the world. How I deal with people from day to day. I grew up a timid child. I remember as a kid being nervous to tell the waiter what I wanted to order off the menu. I was afraid to engage with people. It seems strange that I would end up working in an environment where I was constantly doing just that. In the beginning, I just wanted to make photographs. I chose journalism because there was such a purpose to it. I looked at images in the newspaper and magazines and was overcome by the emotion they showed. I wanted to be a part of that work. Even better, I felt called to do it. When I began learning about journalism in college I was suddenly thrown into this world where things just had to get done. There was no time to be anxious. You had to get out there, ask the questions and create. It was during this time that talking to people, being comfortable, just became second nature. It was as if a switch had flipped. It saved me.

Pro tip

When I was in college I remember being constantly told I would never find a job in photojournalism. Tough to hear because that's all I was interested in doing! Well, it somehow all worked out and I'm exactly where I want to be. My advice is do not let what others tell you is possible or not possible dissuade you. If you want something, go get it. If it doesn't work out, keep trying. And if you're tired of trying, then that's OK too. Follow your gut.

Not long ago, I was photographing a birthday party at a family homeless shelter. The event is thrown by the Birthday Party Project, which offers celebrations for homeless children around the country. There was a moment during the event when I looked over at a 17-year-old girl who was opening her birthday present. The look on her face made my heart smile; these kids aren't used to getting presents. I lifted my camera to photograph her face from across the room. I knew I wouldn't forget her huge smile when she pulled out a bracelet from the gift box, but I wanted to share it so others could see it too. It's a beautiful sense of duty that I'll never take for granted.

The people I photograph. The people I meet. It's them that I think of when I look back on my work. Often, people will comment, "So you just go around taking photos all day?" Pretty much. I tell them my job is going around and observing what other people do with their day. When you think about it, every time I photograph someone, there's a reason for it. I mean, it's news. They could be sitting in a doctor's office waiting to find out if they have cancer, they could be serving life in prison, or they could be taking the Oath of Allegiance at a U.S. citizenship ceremony. With each one of these people I take something with me. A lesson, a reminder or a reality check that I can share with the world. It's a gift. Journalism is a gift. It's my excuse to be curious. To find what drives people. It's in these sometimes long, sometimes brief meetings that I become exposed to all these things I never would have normally known about. A life that is different from my own. A life that awakens my own. It's amazing. And the feeling is something I never anticipated when I decided I wanted to be a photojournalist.

Maybe I was naïve in the beginning, because I had never given much thought to how affected I would be by the people I photograph. There is a part of me that is able to block out emotion and see the world through only my viewfinder, but there will always be a bigger part of me that will be overcome at the end of the day. When the eight-year-old son of a Dallas police officer who was killed in the July 7, 2016 ambush dropped flowers onto his father's grave, I photographed that moment. I knew what I was photographing, but it wasn't until later when I was sitting alone at my desk that I began to feel it. It's in these moments where I have to ask myself why I had to be there with a camera. It's such a personal moment. I don't feel good about getting upset because nothing happened to me, I didn't lose anything. But if I felt something, that means others can too. So I photograph in the hopes that the emotion will spark some sort of something that leads to something good.

At a time when journalism is constantly changing, it's these moments that keep grounded. What I see. The moments. The people. That's why I'm a journalist.

Bio

Rose Baca is a staff photographer at The Dallas Morning News. She joined the News in 2010 to work as a reporter and photographer at its suburban "Neighborsgo" section. In 2014, she moved up to The Dallas Morning News as a staff photographer. She is a graduate of Texas Christian University.

Career timeline

2014–present, staff photographer at The Dallas Morning News.
2010–2014, staff photographer/reporter at "Neighborsgo" at The Dallas Morning News.
2009, graduated from Texas Christian University with degree in news/editorial journalism, photojournalism emphasis.

LEE POWELL

Video reporter

The Washington Post

I didn't get into journalism to save the world.

Or right wrongs.

I report on the world as it is, not as it should be.

What keeps me going through 20-hour days and fading sunsets on freezing hillsides is the greedy desire to know.

I'm greedy because I want to know why a college built a ski hill of fake snow. Why an inn owner is running a newspaper from his front desk. Why people are becoming addicts in a small town. All stories I've done.

I'm greedy for information because our readers and viewers demand it.

The great thing about this business is what you learn. And where you go. My reporting demands I spend little time in a newsroom gathering facts by telephone or online searching. If it doesn't happen in front of my camera, it might as well not have happened.

I talk to people who sometimes don't want to talk — on camera, at least. My job requires the persuasion of a salesman. I go places the public normally cannot: airport ramps, coal mines, a high-security prison, a panda breeding center. My camera becomes the eyes and ears for viewers. I want them to see a jumbo jet settling down on a runway, hear a panda chomping on bamboo.

I started out as a newspaper reporter with a pen and pad. Great writing can reveal a character and re-create a place, but it's a limiting medium without pictures and sound. Still, newspapers did words and television did pictures. Around 2004, it all got scrambled as dial-up internet faded and broadband took hold. Now newspapers were in the video business. I picked up a camera at The Dallas Morning News and started supplementing my print stories with sights and sounds. I taught myself how to edit. I had to learn the visual vocabulary of storytelling with pictures. Photography was not in my background.

But there's that learning bit again. Start telling video stories — many video stories — and the squares and rectangles of an edit eventually fit together into a tale. All the camera angles and moviemaking-in-a-box (eventually a laptop) stand on a foundation that begins with reporting and writing. These are skills learned through effort and experience: how to approach a scene, read a person, make deadline. I see new journalists fresh from graduation brimming with technical know-how but falling short on reporting and writing, especially writing to pictures and sound. You have to write. It's the hardest skill and takes the longest to master. Everything else can be learned.

The way media companies like The Washington Post tell video stories is still being invented. Yet all stories are really same: moments, characters, beginnings-middles-endings. Sometimes the people in our stories can tell the story. But usually they're not professional storytellers. We are. We take viewers by the hand through a maze of information, guiding them with a script of carefully chosen words.

I'm a journalist because of what's revealed when words meld with images and sound. Video storytelling is a visceral medium, revealing joy, anger, reflection, tears.

Pro tip

Never assume anything, from people's motivations to the way they spell their name. Smith could easily be Smythe. Ask and ask again. Check and double-check.

If you're just starting out, you won't get there right away. I'm talking to new grads and old hands learning a new skill. Your footage? Maybe out of focus. Your interviews? Shot against bright backgrounds. Your audio? Fuzzy because you didn't wear headphones to monitor channels 1 and 2. Your edits? Tough since you didn't shoot enough tight shots. Your video stories? Too long. But every story is a learning opportunity. I've edited and reported hundreds of video stories, maybe even a thousand. No two are alike. Every one is a growth opportunity. Go for the small victories, even if it's one nicely framed shot or a single line of script that sparkles.

I'm a journalist because there's a baseline of skills I follow: get it right, be fair, gather edit-able video and clean audio. After that, everything's open to interpretation. You may develop your own style: I like quirky tales. You might have a signature sound if voicing scripts: I'm trying to be less news anchor-like and more conversational. You could develop a specialty: I do longer-term national and investigative stories for now at the Post but I'll gravitate to anything involving airplanes or trains.

You have to read and watch widely. We're talking learning again. I'm in constant story-gathering mode. I've gotten stories from cruise ship dinner guests, a single sentence from an inflight magazine, and just driving around. Whenever I land in a new city, I read the local paper and watch local television news. More often than not, I'll see something that informs the reporting of my story. Go where people gather — but listen more than talk. Use social media as a news wire and tip service, but be wary of sourcing.

My title is video reporter, which means I'm not just a cameraman. My pad and pen just happen to be a camera. The job means early mornings and late evenings to capture good light. Often, I wait for a scene to unfold in front of my lens. Whatever I shoot, I'm thinking how it pairs with words. Is it a beginning? A middle? An end? I keep shooting until I have a closing scene, or several, as options. I knock on doors even if it's late. The evening after the horrific early morning Orlando nightclub shooting, I was on Florida's east coast in the shooter's hometown. I knocked on his sister's door. Which led to another door and a sit-down interview with his father. It was one of the first on-camera interviews Seddique Mateen did. I gave the audio to a print reporter. Then, I edited as fast as I could.

I'm a journalist because I love discovery: where will the story take me next? And if the rest of the media world is already there, how will my story stand out? It's tiring and the burnout risk is high. So sometimes as a journalist, you have to

Source: Jonathan Newton/The Washington Post

say no for sanity's sake. As a former Associated Press colleague tells it, news careers are marathons, not sprints. The people who survive pace themselves.

I'm a journalist doing a job I didn't learn in college. This job at this news organization didn't exist when I was in college. What's changing? Everything and nothing. Formats and delivery channels get ravaged by digital change. Yet people still want stories.

The world as it is. With maybe a glimpse of how it should be.

That's why I'm a journalist.

Bio

Lee Powell is a video reporter at The Washington Post. His stories appear online at washingtonpost.com and in other digital spaces. He shoots, reports, produces and edits his own stories. Powell works most closely with the investigative and national reporting teams at the Post. Stories usually have him on airplanes around the country or sometimes the world.

He has also worked at the Associated Press and The Dallas Morning News doing video reporting and writing for print.

At the AP, Powell was based in Washington, D.C. and was part of an expansion by the news service into video newsgathering for the U.S. market. His stories appeared on broadcast outlets, websites such as The New York Times and online portals like Yahoo!

In Dallas, Powell started reporting in print but was the first metro desk reporter to pick up a video camera in 2005. He became a hybrid reporter, still reporting in print but adding video segments to accompany his own text stories. Powell also worked with other reporters to create video stories.

He has won three National Edward R. Murrow Awards for writing and feature reporting.

Powell's work has been part of other Murrow Awards, Emmys and a Pulitzer Prize. He's also been recognized by the White House News Photographers Association, the National Press Club and the Webby Awards.

Powell graduated from Wheaton College in Wheaton, Ill. where he edited the campus newspaper while also interning in the newsroom of WBBM-TV, the CBS-owned station in Chicago.

Career timeline

2013–present, video reporter at The Washington Post.

2007–2013, broadcast producer/reporter for the Associated Press in Washington, D.C.

1999–2007, staff writer at The Dallas Morning News, including stints at WFAA-TV, the ABC affiliate in Dallas/Fort Worth then-owned by the parent company of the News.

1998–1999, Education reporter at the Wausau (Wis.) Daily Herald. Also co-hosted weekly public affairs program on WSAW-TV (Channel 7), the CBS station in Wausau.

Broadcast journalists

For all the criticism of broadcast journalism, and in particular television news, it is still the most popular medium for news, according to Pew research conducted in early 2016.

When asked what platforms they "often" get news from, 57 percent of respondents said television, which included local, network and cable news outlets. By comparison, 38 percent said online, which included websites, apps and social media; 25 percent said radio and just 20 percent said newspapers.

The numbers show a strong correlation with age. For those 65 and older, 85 percent said they "often" get news from television compared with 27 percent for those 18–29.

The bottom line is that broadcast journalism is fairly stable and strong. Viewers for the network evening newscasts on ABC, CBS and NBC total nearly 24 million a night, up nearly a million from 2008. In 2016, cable news networks CNN, Fox News and MSNBC delivered record ratings.

On the radio side, NPR also has a stable and loyal following with about 26 million weekly listeners, a slight increase from a decade ago.

Many traditional broadcast forms now have broad reach thanks to digital distribution. The popularity of podcasts has given radio broadcasters and others a new outlet for audio content, documentaries are accessible on a wide array of topics via YouTube and Netflix and virtually any news organization can distribute video, including using social tools like Facebook Live.

For local television stations, there is also growth. While the ratings have generally dipped, many stations now produce hours more of news a day than just a few years ago. In 2004, the average local station produced 3.6 hours of news each weekday, a decade later it was 5.3 hours a day with the expansion of morning newscasts to earlier and earlier and the addition of early afternoon news programs.

This is good news for job seekers. In 2015, television stations recorded their second highest employment numbers ever with 27,870 people working in local TV news, according to researcher Bob Papper.

The job of a broadcast journalist, however, is not all glamour, as it may appear. Broadcast journalists have to be just as good at reporting and producing as their counterparts on other platforms, but also need to be able to weave video with words and present it professionally on-air. A lot of work goes into the minute-and-a-half piece you see on TV, yet the power of imagery and the right words can connect with people in a way that is difficult in text.

It's power that has to be carefully used to inform the public instead of just playing to lurid curiosity and sensationalism.

Works cited

Holcomb, J., Matsa, K.E. and Vogt, N. (2016). State of the News Media 2016: Public Broadcasting: Fact Sheet. Pew Research Center.

Mitchell, A., Gottfried, J., Barthel, M. and Shearer, E. (2016). The Modern News Consumer: Pathways to News. Pew Research Center.

Papper, B. (2016). RTDNA Research: Newsroom Staffing.

Pew Research Center. (2016). Network TV: Evening news overall viewership.

Pew Research Center. (2016). State of the News Media 2016: Local TV: Average Number of News Hours Per Weekday.

JOHN SHARIFY

Contributing reporter at KING-TV in Seattle

General manager of Seattle College's Cable Television and Seattle Community Media

As journalists, so often we enter people's lives at either the worst times of their lives or the best times. That opening line you just read is a line I've used before. I'll admit it. In fact, it's how I started a Ted Talk I gave a few years ago about story-telling, about the job we do as journalists.

Here's what I know about me.

I'd prefer the "best times" scenario versus the "worst times" scenario. Any day. But the reality is, most days, we have to cover the bad news. That's what we do in local news. A mother is in grief. Her son has been murdered. "Go cover it!"

And we do.

And we try to get through that day the best we can. It's gut wrenching. We try to not let it get to us. We try. But it does. Of course it does. We're on the front lines of grief after all. "I'm so sorry for your loss," we tell that person we've just met; that person whose life we've entered at the single worst time of their lives.

I'm sure those were the first words out of my mouth when I met Kim Kime. "I'm so sorry …" And I'm sure I was thinking about my own two children the moment she started talking about her son Kris. The thought had to cross my mind, what would I do if I lost my children? Please God, never let that happen to me, like it's happened to this woman I just met.

I'll never forget that day.

I'll never forget that story. It's a story I wanted to share with you because it speaks to why I'm a journalist and why I believe what we do as journalists matters.

The day I met Kim Kime in 2001, I knew the following:

Kim's 20-year-old son had been murdered in Seattle's Mardi Gras riots. Kris was trying to save the life of a woman he didn't even know. And for some reason, someone in the crowd turned on the Good Samaritan and beat him to death. The riots and that murder were captured on video. And now I had the unenviable task of knocking on the door of a grieving mother to see if she would talk to us.

Kim Kime agreed.

Pro tip

Find a mentor who can help you develop as a journalist, someone whose work you admire and you can learn from. I'll forever be indebted to the mentors in my career who pushed me to be better and encouraged me to embrace the craft of storytelling.

Honestly, I don't remember much about that interview, but I do remember what happened right afterwards as we packed up about to head out the door. Kim received a phone call from the local hospital. She was in tears. Tears of joy this time. She could barely get the words out. "A man at Harborview is getting Kris' heart. He's going to get Kris' heart." Larry Levinson was dying and he was about to get the heart of a hero. And I was about to tell a story like I had never told. On the one-year anniversary of Seattle's Mardi Gras riots, my story about Kris Kime aired on KOMO-TV in Seattle. In the report, I said "Kris was a hero for what he did that night, and what he continues to do one year later." It featured the people grateful for Kris' gifts of life; the man breathing Kris' lungs, the woman with Kris' left kidney, the man with his right kidney, the woman with Kris' pancreas and the man with Kris' heart, Larry Levinson. As I write this essay 16 years later, Larry is still alive because of Kris, because of the conversation Kris had with his mom. He had told his mom if anything ever happened to him he wanted his organs donated.

I bet you that conversation was repeated thousands of times after viewers watched the story about Kris Kime. LifeCenter Northwest was flooded with calls from viewers asking how they could become donors too, after watching this story of hope. If you Google LifeCenter Northwest you'll see they're proud of helping "families find meaning in their time of loss."

In fact that's why I do this, to help viewers "find meaning" in the stories I report. In my attempt to do so, I've found meaning in my own life and work.

Bio

John Sharify is a special projects reporter for KING 5 News in Seattle. He's in constant pursuit of meaningful stories to share with his viewers.

Sharify is one of the most honored broadcast journalists in the country, with 63 Emmy Awards and eight National Edward R. Murrow Awards. He received the National Murrow Award for Writing in 2008, 2007 and 2004, which honors the top broadcast news writer in the country. He is also the proud recipient of the 2015 National Press Photographer's Association's Reporter of the Year Award.

In 2012, he received the National Edward R. Murrow award for his documentary "Climb of a Lifetime," which chronicled the lives of recovering addicts training to climb Mt. Rainier. He presented a Ted Talk at TEDxRainier about that climb.

Sharify started his reporting career in New York City at WPIX-TV. In 1989 he headed to the Northwest where he was privileged to deliver his signature life-affirming stories for KOMO 4 News in Seattle for the next 18 years.

When Sharify isn't producing stories for KING, he's helping run two television stations as the general manager of Seattle Colleges Cable Television (SCCTV) and Seattle Community Media (SCM), the city of Seattle's public access station. He's also an independent filmmaker. Sharify directed and wrote the documentary film about the Holocaust "Boys of Terezin," which has been screened in film festivals around the world.

John Sharify is a proud graduate of Princeton University and has a Master of Fine Arts degree in film directing from Columbia University.

Career timeline

2009–present, contributing reporter for KING-TV in Seattle.

2008–present, general manager of Seattle Colleges Cable Television and Seattle Community Media.

2008, contributing reporter for KCTS-TV in Seattle.

1989–2007, reporter for KOMO-TV in Seattle.

1981–1989, producer and reporter for "Best Talk in Town" and news reporter at WPIX-TV in New York City.

MICHELE MITCHELL

Independent documentary filmmaker

I wanted to be the Great American Novelist, even before I heard that cliché. I wrote my first short story at five ("Kitty," the tale of ... a cat), my first novel at 10 ("Kitty," the long version of the tale of a cat), quickly followed by a series of novels about the Easter Bunny, Santa Claus, May the Fairy, Moana (long before Disney had the idea, thank you very much) and, the one I actually learned to type for so that I could bang it out on my mother's manual typewriter at the age of 11: "The Mointer Mansion Adventure." This one starred orphans and — what else? — a creepy abandoned mansion. This one I sent off to a publisher, the one that published my favorite books, the Little House series. Harper & Row turned it down, but very nicely: "This is the best book by an 11-year-old we have read."

Novelists, in art, are always wasting away — either from starvation or tuberculosis or both — in a garret attic. This was not appealing to me. I wrote a letter to a journalist I admired, whose name I seized off the masthead of Sports Illustrated. "What does it take to be a writer?" I asked him. "Are you the daughter of a real estate baron?" he asked in return.

My father reminded me that, in fact, I was not, and that while writing novels was fine, I did need to figure out a way to support myself. I had an excellent option.

Journalists, in art, are always swashbuckling around the world — wiping desert sand from camera lenses, crouching in shelled hotel rooms, and generally committing truth to paper. This seemed a lot more interesting and more likely to pay steadily.

I have now done both: write novels that were actually published, and practice journalism in print, television and film. I have never starved in an attic, and neither have I shaken sand from a camera. But I have realized that, at its essence, there is not much difference between the mediums in motivation for telling a story. It is all about one question: Why did that guy do that to that other guy? There are more sublime ways to phrase that question, but, trust me, that is the fastest one (and in television, "fast" counts).

Pro Tip

Never be afraid to ask a dumb question. Most of your questions are going to sound really stupid anyway, so just do it.

It's an irresistible question, asked in endless variations. Even in the most mundane city council meeting I once attended as an intern for a now-defunct community newspaper, it came up when one old man hit another old man on the head with a stack of file folders. I still couldn't tell you why the one guy hit the other guy, but I can tell you that it led me to check into corruption allegations against a city councilman — allegations that turned out to be true.

What separates the journalist from other media is risk. Often, in order to answer that irresistible question, you have to put yourself out there — way out there. This may come in the form of risk of ridicule, lawsuit, bodily harm or death. And this risk often has very little reward. Journalists spend their careers bearing witness for a world that prefers to look askance. And they do this for a lousy financial upside. No one gets rich — and the ones who you think might be famous are really only famous in a very small circle.

But, answering that irresistible question has two equally irresistible payoffs: it is meaningful, and it is fun. I have done stories that made a viable difference for individuals and for policy. I have caught some very bad people doing very bad things, and they have paid for it as a result. I have seen the worst that people can do to each other, and I have seen the best. I have done shots of vodka with a warlord for safe passage through the Salang Pass; I have eaten bowls of peanuts with the hapless former head of state charged with untangling the Middle East; I have stood in a locker room after Jose Canseco struck out at the bottom of the ninth of the last game of the World Series and seen grown men — millionaires — cry because of this; I have hung out in the shimmering heat of southern Italy with Lou Reed; I have held too many hands in too many refugee camps, swearing that I would find a way to let the world know what I had seen.

I am a journalist because that question never gets old. I will always want to know why. There is the adventure of finding out, knowing that what I am doing may not change anything, but what if it does? Because that's the thing about the practice of factual storytelling: you are either part of history, or you are part of making it.

Bio

Michele Mitchell began her broadcasting career as political anchor at CNN Headline News, where she specialized in U.S. politics. As an award-winning investigative reporter on "NOW with Bill Moyers" (PBS), she developed a reputation for discovering overlooked social justice stories before leaving to start her own company. She has reported from most of the 50 states, as well as the Middle East, North Africa, East Africa, the Caribbean and Southeast Asia. She was the director/producer/writer/co-executive producer of the groundbreaking "Haiti: Where Did the Money Go?" (PBS), which won the 2013 National Edward R. Murrow Award for Best TV Documentary as well as the Gracie Award for Best Investigative Feature and the CINE Special Jury Award for Best Investigative Documentary, among many others. In 2016, her first feature documentary was released in U.S. theaters, the award-winning and universally acclaimed "The Uncondemned."

A graduate of Northwestern University, Mitchell wrote sports for the Chicago Tribune while in college, and she is the author of three books. She began her career on Capitol Hill.

Career timeline

2016, co-director, producer and writer of the documentary "The Uncondemned."

2012, writer, producer, director and co-executive producer of the documentary "Haiti: Where Did the Money Go?" (PBS).

2006, author of "Our Girl in Washington" (Viking).

2004–2006, correspondent for "NOW" on PBS.

2003, author of "The Latest Bombshell" (Holt/Viking).

2000–2003, political anchor for CNN Headlines News.

1998, author of "A New Kind of Party Animal: How the Young Are Changing Politics As Usual" (Simon & Schuster).

1996–1999, freelance journalist for The New York Times, Boston Globe and Washington Post.

1993–1996, communications director for U.S. Congressman Pete Geren.

1989–1992, sportswriter for the Chicago Tribune.

CARLOS C. HOPKINS

Executive producer

KNBC-TV/NBC Los Angeles

I'm a journalist because I have the power to find the truth. I'm a journalist because I can be a voice for someone who can't get any answers. I'm a journalist because people and government need to be held accountable. I'm a journalist because it's a fun job to do.

I didn't know the true power of being a journalist until I became one. I've read about the greats who investigated the Watergate scandal in the 1970s and I listened to TV journalists question presidents during uncomfortable White House news conferences.

But it wasn't until I wrote an editorial while in college at Prairie View A&M University about the deteriorating conditions of its roads that I felt the power. In short, a meeting with representatives from both Prairie View A&M and Texas A&M followed where they addressed the concerns of those roads and promised an action plan. Who knew that my little article that was only stating what other students wanted to say would get so much attention? Imagine what I could do at a reputable news organization with a long list of resources at my disposal.

Managing a group of journalists is a great responsibility. In my case, a group of producers and reporters. I've spent years as a producer writing, showcasing and delivering news through scripts and video. It was my dream job. Now, as an executive producer, it's my dream job on steroids! Yes, I'm stressed 24 hours a day. But, when I get two seconds to think about it, I feel accomplished and feel like I'm having fun.

Walking into the newsroom every day, I look forward to learning something new. There's always something! There are some fierce debates during our editorial meetings. There's laughter, anger, embarrassing moments and a lot of blank stares. But, we always walk away knowing we're going to deliver the most comprehensive news coverage in the market.

Don't let this discourage you. But, I read, at least, 140 scripts each day. I describe it as reading a Harry Potter novel every single day. I'm checking everything from spelling, facts, flow, video, timing and if the anchor team has an equal amount of reads.

Let's take you through a breaking news day. And since this is Los Angeles, I'll use a police chase as an example.

First, there's an assignment desk editor that yells, "I hear a chase on the scanner. We're launching the chopper." I send a producer to the control room and call a director to let them know there's a possibility we're going to break into programming. I then let the anchors know where we're covering the breaking news — it could be the newsroom desk or the main studio depending on the time of day and what we know about the chase. I find at least two people in the newsroom who can quickly turn video based on what happens on TV. Think instant replay during live sporting events. As soon as something visual happens, a video producer turns that video around to get it on the air within seconds. By this time, our digital team is aware of the situation. Depending on what's airing on TV, we could decide to only stream our coverage over the website and news app. We typically treat this as a typical broadcast. But, it's only broadcast over our digital platforms.

Pro tip

It's important to understand people, cultures and areas in your city/country that you're not familiar with. You're fighting to find the "truth" for your viewers/readers. But, you can't fight for "truth" on behalf of people you don't understand.

Next up, check with the assignment desk to see if Closed Captioning has been called.

I then head to the control room to give guidance to the producer and control room based on what we're seeing on the air. This includes: zooming the helicopter camera closer or pulling back, information to put on graphics, information to anchors, should we take this live to the top or bottom of the hour and if/when we go on a delay to keep something gruesome from airing on TV. This can happen multiple times a day. A lot of police chases end before our helicopter gets there.

As a TV manager, there are lots of daily filters one must work through. You have a boss, he or she has a boss, and that person has a boss. You have to make sure you uphold the mission and integrity of your company's news values. Our TV station has to make money for a profit. That's how we're able to bring our viewers the news with the number of resources and skilled journalists.

Depending on the company, upper management is typically transparent about the need to cut back because of a tough financial year. But, those cutbacks should never get in the way of producing great stories. I always say that Edward R. Murrow didn't have half the resources we have today and his reporting was solid. So, if we ever needed to go back to the basics, we could still accomplish our goals.

This job is hard, thankless and you work long hours. So, why do I do this? I'm having the time of my life. Who do you know that can say hundreds of thousands of people get to see your work every single day? Who can say that they are changing policy and making a difference in the lives of so many people every day? It's tough. But, it's a duty. It's my service to my community and my country.

Bio

Carlos C. Hopkins is an executive producer at the West Coast NBC flagship, NBC Los Angeles where he manages a number of producers and writers for the 11 a.m., 4 p.m., 5 p.m. and 6 p.m. newscasts. His experience as a journalist has taken him through newsrooms in Houston, San Antonio, Dallas, Miami and Los Angeles. Hopkins is a graduate of Prairie View A&M University and a winner of multiple journalism awards including Emmy, Regional Edward R. Murrow, National Association of Black Journalists, Associated Press, LA Press Club and Golden Mike awards.

Career timeline

2012–present, executive producer at KNBC-TV, NBC Los Angeles.
2010–2012, executive producer at KTVT-TV, CBS Dallas-Fort Worth.
2007–2010, 11 p.m. producer at WFOR-TV, CBS Miami.
2006–2007, producer at WFAA-TV, the ABC affiliate in Dallas-Fort Worth.
2005–2006, producer at KENS-TV, the CBS affiliate in San Antonio.
2002–2005, producer, writer and production assistant at KHOU-TV, the CBS affiliate in Houston.

WAYNE FREEDMAN

News reporter

KGO-TV
San Francisco

"Why did I ever become a journalist?"

Ever? Did I just write the word, ever?

Yes.

Here it is, again.

Ever.

Become a journalist, and you, too, will ask yourself that question. It will probably come in a moment of tension, doubt, exasperation, exhaustion, frustration, desperation or even physical discomfort.

The last time I asked it, my crew and I were standing in a downpour, getting soaked.

Our assignment desk and producers had tasked us to go live on a Friday night, hours from home. Wind rocked the dish atop our microwave truck. Horizontal raindrops stung our faces like assaulting bumblebees. "What the hell are we doing here?" asked my photographer.

"For the benefit of our loyal viewers, we have become experimental human test strips," I groused back. Then, to the crew watching our signal back in the warm, dry, station, I added wryly, "Yes, this is how you, too, can look if you decide to become a television news reporter!"

What? Were you expecting a rose-colored endorsement of the best job in the world? Apologies. That would be irresponsible reporting.

Why should you ever become a journalist? The best reason would be that you have no choice. The desire to report and tell stories draws you like an irresistible pheromone. That pull defines who you are. It's in your DNA.

In my case, DNA deprived me of math skills and gifted me with words. Language and writing always came easily, even in fifth grade when our English teacher, Mrs. Sherock, would fill her blackboard with weekly vocabulary. "Put those words into a story," she would instruct us.

While classmates struggled, I possessed the uncanny ability to connect all 25 of those unrelated words into one or two brief paragraphs. Can you see how that might translate into being a journalist? If you substitute facts for vocabulary words, it's a valuable aptitude when reporting a story.

Add to that a natural curiosity, an ability to get people to talk, a visual mind, and you have the makings of a television news reporter. "Son, if you want to work in television, do the news," my father advised wisely. "They will never cancel the news." I was a college sophomore at the time, and had pretty much already made up my mind.

The "aha moment" happened in ninth grade. Our school announced the formation of a journalism class for the student newspaper. "They can't do that without me," I thought with a sense of unwarranted entitlement. At 14 years old, journalism already felt like a calling and, in its illusory reality, I convinced myself that the calling needed me. Such feelings of misguided superiority run rampant among journalists. Each of us believes we write and tell better mousetraps than anyone else.

I also learned, early, that journalism is fun. That ninth grade class led to the best beat of all, writing a weekly column about our school in what later became the Los Angeles Daily News. Yes. True. My very first article found its way into a real newspaper. Such reinforcement builds confidence really fast. The columns lasted four years. Writing them provided a degree of independence. While other kids toiled in class, reporting gave me excuses to roam … at least until later, when the Catholic brothers in my high school got wise.

Religion aside, the journalism hall pass lasts for as long as you work. It opens doors while granting a license to ask questions, be a witness, skeptical, suspicious, empathetic, adventurous, informative and enlightening. It provides a lifetime education.

Those are the makings of what we call, "journalistic privilege." Beware, however, that it comes with a price … many prices, actually. Reporting is rarely glamorous, even in television news. Our business is just as Darwinian as the rest of the world, and probably worse. If you want to survive and succeed, stay physically and intellectually fit, be willing to adapt and expect to compete.

Journalism is more than a job. It is a lifestyle and an adventure. Money is important, but it should not drive you. Whether you're just starting out in your career or an established journalist, what matters most in this job is the immense satisfaction of making a good story. If making a good story does not resonate with you, then look for another career.

Success in journalism does not come easily. Not usually, anyway. You'll need to earn it to appreciate it. In the first years of your career, you're likely to become a nomad, moving up to better positions in larger cities. You won't starve, but should not expect to earn much more than a basic living wage. Anticipate 12-hour workdays, sometimes six or seven days a week, including holidays.

Throughout your career, it may seem as if you spend more energy with other people's problems, struggles and triumphs than with your own. If you have a family, you will miss many of your kid's soccer or Little League games. Forget about coaching, especially if you choose broadcast news. When 6 p.m. comes around, you're likely to be tethered to that live signal in the stinging rain.

However, when the journalism bug bites you, it creates odd afflictions with side-effects. If you choose this career, you will cross an invisible line separating life's "civilian" participants from us, the observers. It is an attitude and a philosophy.

You may notice the transformation, someday, when all hell breaks loose at a fire, natural disaster, tragedy or whatever. Facts and people's emotions will channel and flow through you without really sticking. Your professional self will remain mostly detached, allowing you to report impartially. Later, you will leave much of the experience behind.

Police, firefighters and emergency room physicians have the same survival instinct.

This third-person mentality may even appear in your personal life. Who else but a journalist would participate in the birth of his daughter while a small part of him stood back, watched objectively and took mental notes?

Me.

Pro tip

Telling a story is an act of craftsmanship, but don't be obvious about it.

Your hand in the process should remain invisible. Shoot invisibly, write invisibly, edit invisibly and report transparently. If you do a good job, your viewers will never notice your work. They'll just remember the story.

Yes, we're unusual that way. Newsrooms and the journalism tribe possess all the traits of dysfunctional second families. Hopefully you enjoy being around people like us because our chronic qualities include egocentrism, insecurity, self-importance and countless other forms of maladjustment. You will need to make peace with the fact that our industry deals increasingly with people who have predetermined biases. They do not like us, particularly when we challenge those biases with facts.

In television, our viewers have short attention spans. Most news professionals are not proud of that and may even deny it for fear of guilt by association. Quite the contrary — when describing what we do to outsiders, we prefer to make it sound like brain surgery.

Sorry, it isn't. Reporting is just plain hard work.

On a typical day, a television news reporter and his crew do not have time to sit down for a civilized meal. We become experts at scarfing lunches in moving cars, sometimes while steering with our knees. We don't chew. We inhale. This explains why some of us have terrible table manners.

Inexplicably, we love it. We're addicted to deadlines. Being a reporter means performing miracles daily, tirelessly, year after year, for as long as we work, wherever we work, and making those miracles look easy. Brilliance with one story, one day, never carries over to the next. Journalists revel in the challenge of proving themselves with every new assignment. In professional newsrooms, institutional equity rarely exists. We're OK with that. We're wired for it.

When I proposed to my wife, my father offered another sage piece of advice: "The woman you love now is not the woman to whom you will be married years down the road. People change. Circumstances change. Marry someone who you can change with, and who can change with you."

In short, Dad was telling me to marry the heart. My wife, Susan, is a blessing.

Marrying the heart also applies to career choices. Although my heart is in journalism, remember that our business is tied to an ever-changing business world. Our bosses expect us to change with it.

Let's look at the changes in my career.

After that high school newspaper column, I continued to write while at UCLA, worked as a network page production assistant at KABC-TV, and even got an op-ed published in the LA Times.

After earning a master's in journalism from the University of Missouri, I signed on as a photographer at WLKY-TV in Louisville, shooting and cutting on 16mm film. It wasn't an ideal job, but they let me report on weekends, which led to an on-air job across the street at WAVE-TV, a few months later.

Within a year, I moved up to KDFW-TV in Dallas, Texas, as a night reporter.

Ten months later and two years out of school, KRON-TV hired me in San Francisco. I began with general assignment reporting, did investigative, technology and medical beats, and developed a specialty in long-form features, which remain my first love.

In 1989, "CBS This Morning" hired me to travel the country, producing and reporting one big story per week. It was wonderful, but dream jobs rarely last forever, especially when somebody new buys a network and then pays for it by cutting staff.

So, in 1991, I adapted back to daily local news at KGO-TV in San Francisco, earned a reputation for breaking news, and in 2010 came full-circle when the station gave me a video camera to shoot and edit some stories. They use me almost exclusively in the first block. Rather than doing one long, beautiful story per week, it's now two per day, 10 per week, and often more. When you include social media feeds, we essentially report all day on two, three or even four screens via multiple platforms.

The kid who wrote that first newspaper article in ninth grade could never have imagined such a workload. Now, he's geared for it.

My point? Change is constant, meaning that you too will constantly change. Just remember that while our methods of delivering news continually evolve, the elements of a good story remain much the same as they always have.

I view this as a visceral medium. People and emotions put facts into context. When working big stories, I am always looking for revealing, smaller ones inside of them. Conversely, when working a smaller story, I seek the larger truths in life. Viewers remember what they feel. This methodology has served me well.

My reasons for continuing to work as a journalist change with every passing year. After more than four decades, they have become layered and complicated. Stick around long enough, they will for you, too.

I remain a journalist, today, for love of the process and all that comes with it, including travel, variety and honoring the trust that people place in us.

Our daily access to so many places feeds my passion for still photography, which also enhances our social media requirements.

I love the tribal teamwork with managers and especially with my partners in the field. Every assignment is like a buddy trip. We start in the morning with blank sheets of paper and work in a job that plays out like a scavenger hunt. At the end of a day, we have one or two finished stories to show for it.

Finally, as an old-school guy who used to be an obnoxious brat, I like helping the next generation of reporters. Some of them even listen to me.

If you take one truth from this essay, here it is: Most days, our job isn't so much a matter of changing the world as a whole as it is about changing the worlds of individuals, one at a time, and giving our viewers or readers reasons to care or act.

This first hit home in 1991, back in the dream job when I did long-form segments for "CBS This Morning." We traveled to the small border town of Bisbee, Arizona to profile Walter Swan, a most unusual author. Walter was a retired plasterer who, with wife, Deloris, had been married for 50 years and raised nine children.

"Money was always tight," Walter told us. The family never had the internet or even a color television for entertainment, but Walter made up for it by coaxing his kids to bed each night with stories of growing up in Bisbee with his brother, Henry. They were simple stories about his first sighting of an airplane, or how a goat ate his schoolbooks, or about the dark night when his father mistook a jar filled with pond pollywogs for drinking water.

Years later, after the kids moved out, when Deloris and Walter had only themselves and not much to do, she made a suggestion, "Walter, you should take your bedtime stories and write a book."

"But, I can't write," he replied, and it was true. Walter even showed us his old report cards, filled with Ds in English composition.

Still, Walter was a natural-born storyteller, so he rose to the challenge, chicken-scratched his memories at the kitchen table, and Doris corrected his work.

When they finished, the couple sent copies of their manuscript, called "Me 'n Henry" to 14 publishers. They received 14 rejections.

"Still, we had faith," said Deloris. They were naïve, and had courage. So much courage, in fact, that the couple spent much of their life savings to self-publish. "The first time I held that book, I got all choked up," said Walter, who fought tears once again, in describing the moment.

He and Deloris hatched a novel plan. They took their book to the Arizona State Fair and set up a booth. "Meet the author. Get his autograph," Walter pitched.

"Me 'n Henry" sold out.

Encouraged, the Swans printed more books, rented space on Bisbee's main drag, and opened a business called The One Book Bookstore, with hundreds of copies of "Me 'n Henry" piled high.

In that small tourist town, The One Book Bookstore became a grand hit. "It was more money than we'd seen in our entire lives," Doris told us. "I can go to the grocery store, now, and buy anything."

"What is your favorite indulgence?" I asked.

"I just love that artificial crab."

My story about the Swans portrayed optimism, perseverance and success. When you believe in a goal, work at it, and never give up, good stuff happens. That applies to journalism, too.

Change the small worlds, first. Can you guess how Walter's world changed?

Two nights after the Swans appeared on "CBS This Morning," I tuned in to David Letterman's late show. Either he or someone on his staff had seen our segment. And who did Letterman fly to New York City to be his guest?

It was Walter Swan, telling bedtime stories, again, only not to his kids, this time, but to all of America.

He looked like the happiest man on Earth.

Me, too.

So, why did I ever become a journalist? Because, sometimes the simplest of stories provide the most profound of rewards.

Ever?

How about never?

As in, I never considered anything else.

Bio

Wayne Freedman, a 51-time Emmy winner, is a television brat.

His father, Mike Freedman, began with ABC in 1948, and pioneered the use of live, hand-held video cameras for network coverage of news and sporting events. He had his son in the field with him almost as soon as he could walk.

Now, Freedman shoots many of his own stories for the ABC station in San Francisco.

In ninth grade, he published a regular column for what is now The Los Angeles Daily News, and continued it through high school.

Freedman earned a bachelor's degree in political science from UCLA while working as a network page assigned to the newsroom at KABC-TV in Los Angeles. The following year, he finished his master's degree in journalism at the University of Missouri.

He's been on San Francisco television since 1981, beginning at KRON. Before that, he worked at stations in Louisville and Dallas. In 1989, CBS News hired him to produce and report national feature stories for "CBS This Morning."

He returned to San Francisco at KGO-TV/ABC7 in 1991. Since then, he has covered all kinds of local, state, national and international stories. They include Russia's Second Revolution in 1992 and Hurricane Katrina in 2005, along with major fires, earthquakes, elections and NASA space missions. Twice, he crossed the country by train, visiting small towns and taking the pulse of America following the September 11 attacks.

His book, "It Takes More than Good Looks to Succeed at Television News Reporting," now in its second edition, is required reading for major college journalism programs in the United States, Canada and Europe. He has conducted more than 100 narrative writing and visual storytelling seminars for newsrooms and national organizations in the United States and overseas.

His 51 Emmy Awards include 13 for writing, 14 in the category of On Camera News Talent and multiple Emmys in the categories of Breaking News, Feature Reporting, Feature Series, Sports Reporting and News Programming Special. He is also a member of the Northern California chapter's Silver Circle. In 2011, he received his 50th Emmy for shooting and editing his own stories as a multi-media journalist. After the 51st Emmy, he retired from that competition, and now encourages others.

Career timeline

2016, 35th year of reporting in San Francisco Bay Area television. Signed a new, three-year contract.

2012, published second edition of "It Takes More than Good Looks to Succeed at Television News Reporting."

2012, received 50th and 51st Emmy Awards, and retired from competition.

2010, became an MMJ reporter at KGO-TV.

2003, published first edition of "It Takes More than Good Looks to Succeed at Television News Reporting."

1991–present, reporter at KGO-TV, San Francisco.

1989–1991, national feature reporter at "CBS This Morning."

1981–1989, reporter at KRON-TV, San Francisco.

1980, reporter at KDFW-TV, Dallas.

1979–1980, first jobs in Louisville, Kentucky at WLKY-TV (ABC) and WAVE-TV (NBC).

1978, graduated with a Master's in Journalism, University of Missouri.

1977, graduated from UCLA with a bachelor's degree in political science.

1976, first op-ed piece published in the Los Angeles Times.

1974, began work as a production assistant at KABC-TV in Los Angeles.

1969, first article published in junior high school.

Digital journalists

There is no doubt that the future of journalism is in digital. While broadcast and print still deliver more revenue for most traditional news organizations, the trends are clear: the public and advertisers continue to move to newer platforms that evolve daily.

We have seen a dramatic shift in how we consume and create news in the past two decades. Many legacy news organizations underestimated this revolution and were too slow to adjust, relying on their traditional revenue and distribution methods while advertisers and the public moved to websites and later phones, tablets, apps, social media and other new platforms and organizations.

During this reinvention of journalism, entrepreneurs seeking to capitalize on the disruption created digital-native outlets, large and small. Some you are probably familiar with, such as The Huffington Post, BuzzFeed and POLITICO, and many you've probably never heard of because they serve specialized groups, either by location or by topic. Some of those include Insider Louisville (in Kentucky), the Eugene Daily News (in Oregon) and Texas Wine Lover. In addition, several non-profit news outlets now aggressively cover issues of public importance including the Texas Tribune, Inside Climate News, Florida Bulldog and ProPublica.

This means there now many more places to do good journalism. No longer is the career path for journalists limited to covering general news at a small paper or station to start.

Digital news can provide a much more engaging and personalized news experience. New forms such as virtual reality, 360 video and images and searchable databases allow for a powerful connection to news that was simply not possible previously.

At the same time, financial success has not been widespread for these new ventures. BuzzFeed, according to a report, missed its 2015 revenue target by $80 million. Mashable and VICE News both announced layoffs in 2016.

Still, we know the trends and the increase in use of social media for news: 62 percent of adults said they get news from social media in a Pew study, an increase of 13 percent from three years earlier, and the continued reliance on mobile devices, which account for more visits than from desktop for many news organizations, means news organizations have to meet people where they are.

The challenge is developing diverse business models for digital news that will allow news organizations, new and old, to continue to produce good journalism.

Works cited

Gottfried, J. and Shearer, E. (2016). News Use Across Social Media Platforms 2016. Pew Research.

Lu, K. and Holcomb, J. (2016). State of the Media 2016: Digital News Audience: Fact Sheet. Pew Research.

Mullin, B. (2016, April 13). "BuzzFeed's shortfall is alarming, but not apocalyptic, for digital news." Poynter.

Mullin, B. (2016, May 24). "Digital media layoffs continue, this time at VICE News." Poynter.

DAVID COHN

Senior director — Alpha Group

Advance Digital

I distinctly remember my answer as a child when people asked me the obligatory "what do you want to be when you grow up?" question. My answer was not "journalist." At the time, I was dead set on being a stand-up comedian. Robin Williams was my hero.

I can appreciate now my father's response. He didn't panic and tell me that I'd be doomed to a life in cheap bars, living off peanuts and second-hand smoke. Instead, he calmly looked at me and said: "If you want to be a good comedian, you first have to be an excellent communicator. Every comedian is a good writer." I can distinctly remember him over-enunciating the word "comm-un-i-cat-or," exaggerating the movement of his lips as he slowly spoke the word.

I look back on this now and wonder if that somehow steered me into journalism. While my communication is not around humorous topics, I did go into the business of telling the truth to whoever will listen.

It was in college that my pursuit became more consciously directed.

I went to the University of California, Berkeley, which meant there were "unique characters" that would come and go around campus. We had preachers, activists and protestors who would use Berkeley's reputation as a free speech haven to preach their topic de jour.

One of them was a guy named Stoney Burke (you can look him up on Wikipedia). The hair he had left was spiked up and dyed different colors. He wore clothes slightly too big. He was, for all intents and purposes, a clown.

Stoney was a cab driver and actor when he could get a part (he makes a cameo as a truck driver in Matrix Reloaded). Once a week Stoney would take a copy of The Daily Cal and The New York Times and would do a street performance based off the headlines. It was a kind of improv Daily Show, years before Jon Stewart ever pretended to be a news anchor. If you watched Stoney you could tell he was cynical, intelligent, upset and also completely powerless except for his ability to make fun of the headlines to UC Berkeley students. I loved watching Stoney perform.

I am not the only person to have been inspired by Stoney. In San Francisco, November 14, 2007 was declared "Stoney, A Clown Who Rabble Rouses In Defense of Free Speech Day," so obviously he has been recognized for his talents. I can't attribute Stoney with any specific inspiration to get into journalism. I never had any deep conversations with him. There is no mentor/mentee backdrop or context. But Stoney did show me that news is a vehicle for conversation. It's not just ink on dead trees. The ideas presented matter and people can see through bullshit.

But there was no "aha" moment watching Stoney. That required another development during college.

I was a philosophy major, considering pre-law, when a friend roped me into helping out with the undergraduate philosophy journal he had started only a year earlier. It was an entirely student-run show. We raised the money for it, solicited and edited the articles, worked with the printers, learned InDesign for layout and more.

At the end of the ordeal one thing was certain: I never wanted to read another undergraduate philosophy paper ever again.

Pro tip

It is the best of times, it is the worst of times. Some things change and some things stay the same. Now I know, and knowing is half the battle. Above all, don't plagiarize.

But there was definitely something about the process I loved. So, I looked for something similar to dive into.

From there I found myself working on the undergraduate literary arts publication on campus. Once again, a student-run show from start to finish. But the content left me wanting. It was poems, short stories and other acts of fiction. All fine and dandy, but not something that really got me up in the morning.

But something kept me moving forward and overall happy with the endeavor. There was something in both the philosophy and literary arts journals that I wanted to keep pursuing.

So I volunteered to write for the student newspaper on campus. I didn't write much. I wasn't a "full-time" staffer like some of the other students. But every piece left me fulfilled. This is what I was looking for. I knew I wanted to be a journalist.

But why?

I was interested in the flow of information. For me, everything boiled down to information being exchanged. Physical bodies in motion, genetics, all the way up to abstract ideas — everything was about the exchange of information and pushing forward. Human intelligence, in this framework, was one of the highest forms of harnessing and sharing information, because we could store and manipulate the information.

But here's the catch. I wasn't interested in sharing just any old information. I wanted it to have caveats. The information had to be true and accurate to the best of my knowledge. The information had to be collected ethically and honestly. These are the caveats of journalism. I didn't like the philosophy journal because it had no practical value for people and the literary arts journal was mostly fiction. But the student newspaper hit all the right buttons for me.

Now I just had to push forward.

That wasn't easy. I was a "professional intern" for a year and a half at least, getting by on minimum wage and whatever I could scrounge up.

Why would anyone do this? Or more specifically, why would I do this?

Everyone has a bit of an idealist inside of them somewhere. When we tell younger people to pursue their dreams, what we really mean is "do what you think will make the world better." If somebody really pursues what they think will improve the world, they'll enjoy it more than anything else.

And that is a unique question for everyone. What will make the world better? For some the answer might be becoming a teacher, doctor, police officer or more. I remain interested in how people communicate. Not just in daily conversations or even in the written word, but the systems by which this happens.

And if that is your interest, this is an amazing time to be alive and do journalism.

Bio

In the last decade, David Cohn has been at the forefront of innovation in journalism. During his career he has worked on some of the first experiments in distributed reporting, social journalism, citizen journalism and structured journalism. In 2008 he created the first platform to crowdfund journalism. In 2010 he was named one of the "Ten Under 30" by Folio magazine and in 2013 Columbia's Journalism School gave him the Alumni Innovation Award.

Today he is a senior director at Advance Digital's Alpha Group, which does in-house incubation for the media organization. This comes on the heels of his time as an executive producer at AJ Plus, part of Al Jazeera's research and development team, leading efforts to turn a broadcast organization into a digital operation.

Before that he was the chief content officer of Circa, a startup redefining how news is consumed on the mobile phone and one of the first organizations to experiment with atomized news structures or "object-oriented journalism."

Cohn has written for Wired, Seed, Columbia Journalism Review and The New York Times, among other publications.

He has been a lecturer at UC Berkeley's journalism school and was a fellow at the University of Missouri Journalism School's Reynolds Journalism Institute. He serves on the board of several journalism organizations including the Global Editors Network, The San Francisco Public Press and the Online News Association.

Career timeline

2015–present, senior director of Alpha Group at Advance Digital.
2014–2015, executive producer at AJ+.
2012–2015, chief content officer of Circa.
2008–2012, founder and executive director of Spot.Us.

MILA SANINA

Executive director and editor

PublicSource in Pittsburgh, Pennsylvania

 It all started with a nose. It was a big nose for a little person. My mom talks about my nose all the time when recounting memorable moments of my first days of life: "All you could see was your nose. I didn't know where it came from, I thought it's going to be a problem forever — oh how unfortunate, her nose is bigger than everything else on her face."

My nose never grew in size, it grew into an adjective. In kindergarten, I was called "nosey"; in school, I wrote for a school newspaper and yes, nosey, I was. I wrote about classes, teachers and at times I even wrote provocative poems. I got in trouble for writing them. Not with teachers. With classmates. They didn't like me writing satirical poetry about them, everyone else thought the poems were fair. Pursuit of fairness is why I am a journalist.

The sense of injustice whether it was in school or in the community has always been a driving force for me. I hated it when my peers would ask me if they could copy homework from my notebook or cheat on the exam. I felt it was wrong and spoke out about it. Others considered it a betrayal. I learned it early: being nosey and speaking out were not strategies to win friends or approval. That's why I am a journalist, I suppose.

I was lucky, very lucky to have been born to a mother who cared about education, and to a father who was an artist. I was lucky to get a decent school education and learn English. My only misfortune was to have been born in the Soviet Union and raised in the independent country of Kazakhstan, a country where being a journalist is a life-threatening profession.

Before the opportunity of being a journalist materialized for me, I tried to abandon that idea altogether, several times. But when you go against your true nature, you become miserable. I knew the joy of being a reporter, the joy of playing with words, talking to people. I came to Pittsburgh in 2008 to do my master's at the University of Pittsburgh. The degree was in global political economy at the Graduate School of Public and International Affairs. I loved the school and still found ways to write about policy with a journalistic eye.

But I wanted to do more, to write more, to do interviews, to share people's stories. To me, it was tantamount to making a difference in the world, to make it better, to give people an opportunity to empathize or disagree or learn and perhaps, even move them to action — that's what journalists do, right? The opportunity to do that in the U.S. thanks to the First Amendment should not be wasted. It's priceless, the fact that journalists can do it here without fear or favor.

Journalism wooed me back. It happened fast: first, CNN, then the PBS News-Hour. After that, I came back to Pittsburgh and landed a job at the Pittsburgh Post-Gazette, where I worked for five years and where my last post was as deputy managing editor.

Pro tip

Be bold, be thorough, be patient and remember: you cannot cry until you try.

I am glad journalism took over my career path. I love my work. I love how every day I am challenged to keep my mind open, to keep my notebook nearby and always have a pencil that works.

As a journalist, you are guaranteed to meet fascinating people, witness historic events, solve puzzles, whether it's about structure of a piece or a challenge to explain complex issues to your readers. These are good enough reasons to be in the profession, as agonizing as it may be.

There is a sense of mission to being a journalist. Yes, it's all those true statements that sound very cliché today. "Afflict the comfortable and comfort the afflicted" is one of them. But there is more. Freedom of the press is not just the lifeblood of democracy forcing accountability and transparency; Thomas Jefferson himself once said, "It is also the best instrument for enlightening the mind of man, and improving him as a rational, moral, and social being." That's why I am a journalist.

It is a magical feeling when you write a story and hear from a source or from a reader or your story makes changes happen, even if these are small changes that inspire conversations or form a network. It's public-service journalism when you right the wrongs, when you ease the pain, when you give voice to people who feel disenfranchised, ignored, underprivileged and forgotten.

It's not easy to be in journalism these days, especially when assaults on reason get more frequent and the business models for sustaining legacy media are crumbling. It's off-putting when the winner in the online space is an outlet that publishes fake news and gets the most likes and pageviews, no matter the quality, veracity or substance of the reporting. But despair tends to paralyze and it's not a solution. The good news is that there is hope. Not an unabashed kind — that sort of hope can be as calcifying to creativity as despair can — but healthy inquisitive hope. Hope that solid needs-based local reporting will survive and thrive because narrative storytelling, partnered with community involvement and active listening is a no-brainer. There are models out there that work. And I want to make it work, to make sure journalism survives. Our democracy depends on it.

At a time when our community feels more alienated by "the media" and there is a sense of resentment towards reporters, it's more important than ever to show what good journalism represents and what it can do. We need to be aware of the opportunity that independent journalism and unbiased coverage, the kind my team at PublicSource provides, can give to our community and the country in general. It can inform and educate. It can inspire change. It can protect the afflicted and hold those in power accountable. That's why I am still in journalism.

And lastly, journalists are the best colleagues on earth: they are driven, inspiring, witty and often sarcastic. They are always busy but most of them make the moments that they have count. At times you may be lucky to work with a reporter who teaches you to appreciate the rhythm of a good story, an editor who breathes a sense of mission into you, teaches you to be your own Strunk and make every word count. It's wonderful there are still editors who have those values, appreciate perfection, recognize and fight against mediocrity. I strive to do that every day. And it's worth it.

Bio

Mila Sanina is the executive director and editor of PublicSource, a journalism nonprofit focusing on in-depth reporting for the Pittsburgh region. Previously, she was the deputy managing editor at the Pittsburgh Post-Gazette, where she led innovation in storytelling and worked on integration of print and online operations, she edited stories, occasionally fixed typos, read online comments on post-gazette.com (yep!) and fought with its CMS. At the PG, she was a co-creator of The Digs, the project that gave a new life to the old photos never digitized before. Prior to joining the Post-Gazette, Sanina worked at the PBS NewsHour exactly at the time the Arab Spring began, gathering information from Tunisia, Libya and Egypt, and before that, at

CNN International, where she was an assignment editor at the international desk, the job that involved working with 26 international bureaus, gathering stories and coordinating the supply of content from all over the world to CNN's U.S. shows. Sanina was born in the Soviet Union and grew up in the independent country of Kazakhstan, but Pittsburgh owns her heart. "It's a perfect place for journalists. The city is full of characters and surprises ... and most importantly, it appreciates a good story." Sanina holds a master's degree from the Graduate School of Public and International Affairs at the University of Pittsburgh.

Career timeline

2016–present, executive director and editor of PublicSource in Pittsburgh.
2015–2016, deputy managing editor of Pittsburgh Post-Gazette.
2013–2015, assistant managing editor of Pittsburgh Post-Gazette.
2011–2013, social media editor at the Pittsburgh Post-Gazette.
2011, desk assistant at the PBS NewsHour.
2010, assignment editor at CNN International.

STEVE MYERS

Editor of The Lens

New Orleans

I got into journalism in high school because I liked to write. But it took a while for me to figure out why I wanted to write.

I remember driving home from my first public meeting. It was somewhere outside Charleston, West Virginia, where I had been hired at my first newspaper job. I was the labor and environment reporter, and I can assure you I knew little about either when I was hired.

This meeting was about flooding problems related to development. People were riled up. One after another, they shared stories of being flooded in rainstorms because of development on the mountainside above.

I bounced along the interstate in my 20-year-old rusted pickup (first journalism jobs don't pay well) thinking about the meeting. On the surface, it had been about rainwater, but those testimonials showed it was about something deeper: suffering; frustration with lack of law enforcement; people being higher, literally and figuratively, than others. I was excited and nervous, unsure if I could convey that.

"You'll be paid in ways other than money," Chip Scanlan, my mentor in a postgraduate program at the Poynter Institute, had told me a couple months earlier. That's what someone told him as a young reporter, and he passed it down to us.

It's true: As a journalist, you get to sit in the front row of history. But you also sit in the front row of everyday life: trials, school board meetings, public forums. To some people, those run-of-the-mill events are just as important as the history-making ones.

I've attended a lot of meetings that I never would have attended if I didn't have to. I've talked to many more people who are different from me, because you can't write a story with an empty notebook (I've tried). I've gone places where I had no business being, except that it was my job.

Along the way, I've learned what it means to participate in a democratic, capitalist society.

Wherever I've lived, there's a direct correlation between how informed I've been as a citizen and how much I've interacted with the community as a journalist. I've never been more connected to my community than when I was a local government reporter, regularly talking to politicians, lawyers, bureaucrats, gadflies, rabble-rousers and all the ordinary people in between.

There are all kinds of friction points between people in a community, whether they're packed into apartment buildings or spread out across the plains. Many seem trifling, unless it's your sidewalk, your school crossing, your stream. Most people don't even think about these things until it affects them — and then they don't know where to turn. Sometimes they turn to a reporter.

All my life, I've wanted to know how things work. As a kid, I took electronics apart to see what was inside. I learned how engines work by buying a motorcycle that didn't run and figuring out how to fix it.

As a journalist, I get paid to figure things out. In essence, I'm a professional citizen. Are you frustrated that your sidewalk is broken? I know whose job it is to fix that. What exactly do your property taxes pay for? I can tell you. What can you do about the bus that barrels down your street every afternoon? I know who to call. Does your school have to do more to help your struggling kid? I bet I know who can tell you.

Pro tip

Do the work. No one who's truly excellent got that way on talent alone.

Journalists ask questions about things like sidewalks and schools, but the answers we seek are broader than any single problem. Who made the rules? Who wins and loses? Why is it this way? Is there another way? These inquiries are part of our compact with the public; it's why our profession is included in the Constitution.

Journalists have many privileges. People save seats for us. They let us hook up our computers to their Wi-Fi. We get to talk to people who don't make time for just anyone. All these things can be taken away.

But some things can't be — the rights afforded to any citizen. Much of what journalists do is exercise those rights. Anyone can attend a city council meeting. Anyone can go down to the police station and see a report. Anyone can look at work orders in the city streets department.

Journalists are better at doing those things because they're more experienced. But the biggest difference between me as a journalist and most citizens is what I do with this information. I'll tell you everything I learned, but I'll hold back on what I think about it. The more I voice my opinion, the less valuable I am to a news organization. That's not because it colors my work (whether I voice them or not, I have opinions), but because it colors how people will perceive it.

This is controversial, especially now. Like everyone else these days, journalists are encouraged to share their every thought. For some people, withholding judgment is a deal-breaker. They start out as journalists, but they leave after a few years to become activists, work for government or go to law school. Journalism provides an excellent foundation for those careers.

Sometimes it's hard to be on the sidelines. But the 2016 presidential election showed me that speaking your mind is just one way to be civically engaged.

Before you act, you need to know what's going on. What's a reliable source of information? What widely held beliefs have no basis in fact? What point of view does that news site have? Is that a real news story or a hoax crafted for financial gain? Too often, people make up their minds without asking these questions first.

This isn't new, but now it's everyone's problem. Before the web and social media, there were relatively few producers of information and lots of consumers. Being a smart news consumer benefited you and maybe the people closest to you, but that's it.

Now there is no "mass media" to shape a common understanding of the world. Media is becoming more fragmented. Traditional local news sources have atrophied. I'm part of that shift. I started at a newspaper; now I work at a nonprofit news site. The Lens does the in-depth, policy-oriented stories that newspapers once showcased every Sunday.

In this world, the average citizen has as much power to spread information and misinformation as me — maybe more, if he or she is really popular on Facebook. I don't expect everyone to start reporting on city council meetings. But people can take greater responsibility for what they consume and share.

The 2016 presidential election showed many voters are living in parallel information universes, hearing completely different versions of the same events, reading fake news stories and repeating debunked claims.

President Donald Trump waged an unprecedented war on the press, often turning the crowds at his rallies against reporters and photographers. Journalists were kept in a pen, unable to mix with his supporters. That probably contributed to the media's underestimation of the movement that swept Trump into the White House.

Source: Photo courtesy of Della Hasselle

The message was clear: Those people in the pen aren't like the rest of us. CNN's Brian Stelter responded to this idea the day before the Electoral College convened: "Don't let government devalue and delegitimize journalism, because press freedom is your freedom."

Journalists like me are happy to exercise that freedom on behalf of the majority of people who won't. We'll be your professional citizens. But you, too, should participate in democracy by applying some critical thinking to what you watch and read. Even if you're not a journalist, you can start acting more like one.

Bio

Steve Myers is editor of The Lens, a nonprofit, in-depth newsroom in New Orleans. He's worked for The Lens in some capacity since 2012, guiding reporters as they delve into stories about government accountability, charter schools and Louisiana's eroding coast. For two of those years, he was professional-in-residence at Texas Christian University's journalism department, where he taught online journalism practices and supervised senior-level projects. He supervised and edited The Lens-ProPublica collaboration "Losing Ground," an interactive examination of coastal loss that won eight national awards and was a finalist for several others.

Before moving to New Orleans in 2012, Myers was managing editor of Poynter Online, where he wrote about emerging media practices such as citizen journalism, nonprofit news sites, real-time reporting via social media, data-oriented news apps, iPhoneography and the fact-checking movement. His essay on fact-checking was published in "The New Ethics of Journalism" in 2013.

He spent about nine years at newspapers, including five as a local government reporter in Mobile, Alabama. He was a 2006 Ohio State University Kiplinger Fellow and an Open Society Institute Katrina Media Fellow. He's spoken at South by Southwest Interactive twice, once about fact-checking and once with the man who live-tweeted the raid on Osama bin Laden's compound.

Myers is married with two children, an old house and two motorcycles that don't get out much. He's probably drinking coffee right now.

Career timeline

2016–present, editor of The Lens in New Orleans.

2014–2016, professional-in-residence in the journalism department at Texas Christian University.

2014–2016, special projects editor, The Lens.

2013–2014, managing editor, The Lens.

2012, senior staff writer and deputy managing editor, The Lens.

2009–2012, managing editor, Poynter Online.

2008–2009, news editor, Poynter Online.

2007–2008, web producer, Poynter Online.

2006–2007, Open Society Institute Katrina Media Fellow.

2006, Ohio State University Kiplinger Fellow

2001–2005, county government reporter at the Press-Register in Mobile, Alabama.

2000–2001, night police reporter at The News & Observer in Raleigh, North Carolina.

2000, co-founded y2kWhistlestop.com and traveled the country covering the presidential primaries.

1997–1999, labor and environment reporter, Charleston Daily Mail in Charleston, West Virginia.

1997, Poynter Institute postgraduate fellowship.

Journalism leaders

Here's your job: manage a rapidly changing business with financial turmoil, intense competitive pressures and a barrage of attacks from the public. Welcome to news management. Don't expect a lot of thank-you notes.

Leading a news organization these days is not easy. There is no way around that.

However, for the right people, this is a time when you can make a lasting impact helping a legacy newsroom survive and thrive in the digital age or you can reimagine journalism and launch something completely new.

It should go without saying, but I'll put it on the record here, that the essential trait for a news manager regardless of platform or management level is a deep commitment to the best ideals of journalism. If you want examples of that check out two Oscar-winning films from four decades apart, "Spotlight" (2015) and "All the President's Men" (1976). You're likely to have seen these movies, and I hope you paid attention to the fact that the reporters at the heart of those stories were able to do their important work because of the steadfast backing of their editors. The bosses didn't shy from conflict or criticism, but, instead, pushed their reporters to dig deeper.

Of course, many excellent news managers have never been portrayed by the likes of Liev Schreiber and Jason Robards. Most toil away in relative anonymity. We don't often read their bylines or see them on television, yet their work and commitment is central to good journalism.

In an era of corporate consolidation, it's not just local editors, producers and other managers who are responsible for keeping journalism the focus, but also executives at the parent companies whose reach can stretch across newsrooms from coast-to-coast.

With much of the public disillusioned and disconnected from journalism, it is incumbent upon those with the power to guide these organizations to do so in a manner that will regain the public's trust.

The best news managers bring a strong vision, a zeal for the best ideals of journalism, understanding of the community they serve and a keen sense of the business and where it's going.

AMINDA (MINDY) MARQUÉS GONZALEZ

Executive editor and vice president for news

Miami Herald

Source: Miami Herald

I came of age in Miami during the turbulent 1980s, when the headlines in my local paper relentlessly chronicled the growing pains of a fast-changing city.

Public corruption was endemic, from the school board superintendent who used taxpayer dollars to live lavishly — including gold fixtures in his bathroom — to the county manager charged with buying expensive, stolen suits at cut-rate prices.

It was the heyday of the Cocaine Cowboys and the drug wars played out in public, from a deadly shoot-out in the parking lot of a popular mall to the bales of marijuana found floating in canals or dropped from helicopters in suburban backyards.

And the city roiled with ethnic and racial tension.

One month into the 1980 Mariel Boatlift that would bring thousands of Cubans across the Florida Straits to Miami, an all-white jury acquitted four Miami-Dade police officers accused of beating to death a black insurance salesman. The neighborhood burned for three days and 18 people died.

That was the backdrop to my high school days.

By then, I knew that I wanted to be a journalist. A middle school teacher had made the suggestion after I turned in an essay on "The Diary of Anne Frank." I joined the school newspaper and found my calling.

There was only one place I wanted to work and that was at my hometown newspaper, the Miami Herald. I began as a college intern in the summer of 1986. My first assignment was in the community news bureau, writing features about locals — like the woman who won the Betty Crocker cooking contest and the man who had turned a woodworking hobby into a small enterprise.

Soon, I cut my teeth covering a small city, one of the poorest in South Florida. It didn't take long to find stories of malfeasance.

The home phone bills of the mayor and commissioners, paid by the city, included expensive long-distance calls to relatives and pay-per-minute calls to the "Love Line" and the "Pisces Line." On-duty police officers were tapped to chauffeur elected officials to events, often outside the city limit. Then one of my best sources called to give me a scoop: She had been stealing worker compensation checks from city employees to help pay for a drug habit.

It was difficult work. Two years out of college, I was a Hispanic woman covering a predominantly black community. During one public meeting, the mayor called me a racist. But the residents, whose hard-earned taxes were being squandered, thanked me.

That's when my role became clear to me: I worked for the people. I represented their interests. I could give voice to their concerns when no one else did.

Twenty-four years after starting as a rookie reporter, I was named executive editor of the Miami Herald.

Pro tip

We need journalists who can shoot and edit videos, who are adept at social media, who can FB live. But none of that matters if you are not a great reporter. That's the most important element and it is sometimes lost with all of our new gadgets. Stay curious. Be inquisitive. Be industrious. Dig, dig, dig. And unlike other professions, reporting is a craft. The more you work at it, the better you'll become. Start as soon as possible with internships. No one should graduate college without at least one internship.

It is an incredible honor and an awesome responsibility.

For more than a century, the Miami Herald has covered this city with courage. I inherited a strong tradition of journalism excellence. Through our reporting, two wrongfully convicted men were freed from Florida's Death Row. We detailed the U.S.–Iran-Contra connection. We were the lifeline for the community after Hurricane Andrew, then examined how lax zoning, inspection and code enforcement contributed to the destruction.

I am a steward of that legacy.

The headlines continue to sound familiar.

New waves of Latin American immigrants seek refuge in Miami from political turmoil, most recently from Venezuela.

Source: Miami Herald

An unarmed, black teenager from Miami is killed in Central Florida by a self-appointed neighborhood watchman, laying the foundation for a national outcry that became Black Lives Matter.

In the past few years, three local mayors and a city manager have been arrested on corruption charges. In that small, impoverished city I once covered, two reporters have spent a year uncovering a string of corruption that has driven the city to the brink of bankruptcy.

These are stories that would not come to light if it weren't for the dedication and persistence of reporters for whom this is a calling.

Our core mission has never been more critical or imperiled.

It is a difficult time to be a journalist. We are forging a new path and it's still not clear what lies ahead.

Yet this is an exhilarating time to be a journalist. The same technology that is disrupting the business model is giving us myriad ways to tell stories and reach readers.

Every day is an opportunity to make a difference. Few people have the privilege to do work that matters.

Sometimes it stems from a small story, maybe the brief about a hit-and-run that results in a reader tip to police. Then there is the life-changing work: the year-long investigation that details the deaths of hundreds of children who died within Florida's child welfare system, leading to laws being changed.

We must continue to hold the powerful accountable, to tell the stories of those who have no voice, to expose the dark corners of our communities, to inform and cut through the overwhelming clatter of misinformation and lies.

That is why I became a journalist. This is why I am still a journalist.

Bio

Aminda (Mindy) Marqués Gonzalez is executive editor and vice president for news at the Miami Herald.

Born in New York to Cuban immigrant parents, Marqués began her career as an intern at the Miami Herald and rose through the ranks to become the paper's first Hispanic editor in 2010. She is also only the second woman to hold the post.

Her career has included assignments as a metro reporter, assistant city editor and deputy metro editor, directing the Miami Herald's local, state and community news operations. She left the paper in 2002 to work as Miami bureau chief for People magazine, overseeing coverage for the southeast U.S., the Caribbean and Latin America.

She returned to the Miami Herald in 2007 as a multimedia editor. She later was promoted to Sunday/features editor, senior editor for news and managing editor before becoming executive editor in November 2010.

During her tenure, the Miami Herald has been a Pulitzer Prize finalist three times. As managing editor, the Herald was breaking news finalist for its 2010 coverage of the earthquake in Haiti that claimed 300,000 lives. In 2012, the Miami Herald was a finalist in public service for an investigative series detailing Florida's systemic failures in regulating assisted-living facilities. In 2016, the Herald was a Pulitzer Prize finalist in local reporting for a series that detailed a local drug sting operation that cost millions but yielded no arrests.

The Miami Herald has won 20 Pulitzer Prizes in its history.

Marqués is a 1986 graduate of the University of Florida, where she was honored as an Alumni of Distinction by the College of Journalism and Communications in 2012.

She serves on the board of the Pulitzer Prize, is a member of the National Advisory Board of the Poynter Institute, sits on the board of the Associated Press Media Editors and is the current president of the Florida Society of News Editors. She is also on the advisory councils of the Journalism and Women Symposium and the Lillian Lodge Kopenhaver Center for Women in Communication at Florida International University.

As executive editor of the Miami Herald, Marqués has oversight and responsibility for the newspaper's print and online news operation, which reaches 1.2 million readers a week.

During nearly a decade of local reporting, Marqués went on to cover Hialeah, the second largest city in the newspaper's home county, and followed the landmark case involving the Santeria religion to the U.S. Supreme Court.

Marqués and her husband have two children.

Career timeline

2010–present, executive editor and vice president for news.

2010, managing editor of the Miami Herald.

2009–2010, senior editor, news at the Miami Herald.

2008–2009, Sunday/features editor at the Miami Herald.

2007–2008, features editor at the Miami Herald.

2007, associate editor/multimedia at the Miami Herald.

2002–2007, Miami bureau chief for People magazine.

2001–2002, deputy metro editor at the Miami Herald.

1997–2001, assistant city editor, urban affairs/day slot at the Miami Herald.

1995–1997, assistant editor/neighbors at the Miami Herald.

1986–1995, reporter covering government, Hispanic affairs and general assignments at the Miami Herald.

PETER BHATIA

Editor and vice president

The Cincinnati Enquirer

Source: The Cincinatti Enquirer

I discovered journalism as a kid.

I published — and I use the term loosely — a neighborhood newspaper when I was about 12. It featured insightful narrative reporting about what my buddies and I were doing during a summer break. It included stories illegally reproduced from one of the local papers where I lived in Pullman, Washington. I didn't know any better.

My dad ran it off for me on a ditto master at his office at Washington State University. All 20 copies or so off it. In a fit of ego long discarded it was named "The Bhatia Tribune." I am fortunate that no copies survive. Someone today might tweet that it was failing and sad.

It's hard to imagine this childhood journalistic effort led to 40-plus years in journalism, but it probably did. From there it was my high school paper — believe it or not it was named the Hi Times, and yes, this was the 1960s. I wrote for my college paper, the Stanford Daily, although I was so busy experiencing college in multiple ways I was never a top editor. I interned between my junior and senior year of college at The Spokesman-Review in Spokane. It was summer of 1974 and Richard Nixon resigned. I remember bringing the little black-and-white TV I had in my apartment into the newsroom so we could watch the proceedings.

But it wasn't Watergate that brought me to journalism. It was the realization that telling stories and writing about interesting events (if you thought high school sports was interesting) was a form of public service. It was a way to make a difference. It was a way to do good.

The event that probably sealed my fate as a journalist was sometime in early 1975. At the time I was considering grad school in journalism, getting an MBA or going to law school. As I walked out a classroom at the History Corner at Stanford after taking the law boards I said to my classmate and friend Mike Lopez: "Well, I'm going to have a great career in journalism."

Mike recalled this event, much to the amusement of classmates and me, at our 40th reunion in 2015. He quoted me accurately.

Please don't misunderstand. I was keeping my options open, but I knew deep down inside that journalism was where I belonged. It is still the case today. Why I am a journalist has evolved over the decades and was brought into sharp relief by events around the presidential election of 2016. But this much hasn't changed: It was and is still a way to do good. To be a public servant. To make a difference.

After my undergraduate days I was on my way to the Medill School of Journalism to get a master's degree in journalism to go with my history degree from Stanford. My late father was an academic and a Ph.D. so it made sense I would at least get an advanced degree. But journalism intervened.

The Spokesman-Review called and I was off to begin my career. I deferred my admission to Medill for a year. But after a year I was having so much fun working as a reporter and copy editor in Spokane that I bought a new car instead of going to grad school. I never made it, although I am thrilled to be able to give back late in my career in teaching journalism ethics at Arizona State's Cronkite School and in the journalism school at the University of Cincinnati.

Pro tip

Make sure you master the basics — there is no substitute for the ability to write and report. But the successful journalists of today must also master all the digital skills. Some of that is easy for you: shooting photos with an iPhone, social media, etc. But you must also have video shooting and editing skills, knowledge of fundamental web work and more. When you have the chance, outwork everyone else. Volunteer for anything. Show what you can do.

My career has taken me throughout the country. I spent 10 years at the San Francisco Examiner, rising to deputy managing editor. I was managing editor of the Dallas Times Herald and Sacramento Bee. I was editor of the York (Pa.) Dispatch and Sunday News. I spent 21 years at The Oregonian in Portland as managing editor, executive editor and editor. My most recent posting is as editor and vice president of audience development at The Cincinnati Enquirer and Ohio editor for Gannett's USA Today Network.

Early on, I just wanted to be a great reporter. I wanted to tell stories. I wanted to be a foreign correspondent. But early on bosses figured out I had a gift for editing and that grew into leadership. As a result I've spent roughly 36 of my 41 years leading journalists, not producing journalism.

But the practice of journalism is still in my heart. It makes me who I am. With my family, it shapes my worldview. And it drives me to do good.

I take my responsibility as a journalist very seriously.

I tell groups when I am speaking that the press is the only profit-making institution protected by the Constitution. Even though that freedom is under attack in 2016, it remains a fundamental of our society and that drives me to make sure our journalism is of the highest quality.

So I am a journalist because I honor the freedoms that define our nation and because I believe so strongly that our freedoms don't come without continuing to protect, enforce and live them. The First Amendment is more than its 45 words. It isn't hyperbole to say it sets our base as a nation. It defines us as a nation of ideas, of free and independent thought, of one in service to the citizenry and with a free and independent press that watchdogs all we are.

I drummed the five tenets of the First Amendment into my two children when they were young. I told them it was so important they knew what they were and what they meant. The vast majority of Americans can't name the five tenets — press, speech, religion, right of assembly and right to petition the government. Neither is a journalist; but they are both fine young adults, who recognize our freedoms as sacrosanct and who define the best of who Americans are. I realize browbeating my children about the First Amendment won't win any parenting awards. But they get why I did it.

I am a journalist, it also turns out, because I like working with journalists. I like people who like to dig for stories. Who are skeptical about what the powerful feed us. Who are not afraid to challenge convention. Who care about those who have less in our society. And most importantly, who share my passion and deeply held conviction about telling the truth — wherever our reporting may lead us.

I also became a journalist because it is fun. In what other field do you have the opportunity to witness history being made so close to the action? I was on the streets for riots in San Francisco. I had the opportunity to cover the turbulent times in Central America in the 1980s. I was inside the ropes to see a young phenom named Tiger Woods win the U.S. Amateur. And most of all I have been doing what I did best: coordinate, conceive and execute substantial journalism in newspapers and today in all the digital forms we now have available. I didn't really understand that was my purpose or my gift, but it has given me such incredible experiences.

And today, in the latter stages of my career I am a journalist so I can fight for journalism and the kind of journalism that must define us. That means a journalism that values accuracy, completeness and balance. I believe many of us are stunned by what has played out in the 2016 election. Fake news, the press portrayed as a villain, the refusal to answer legitimate questions from the press, etc. I attended a Trump rally in Cincinnati and witnessed the open derision towards the media. (For the record, I applauded when the national press walked in.) My email and phone calls have been brutal, especially after the Enquirer endorsed Hillary Clinton, the first Democrat endorsed by the paper in a century.

We live now in a society where truth doesn't matter, many have written. I cannot go there. Yes, we have work to do to help the country see the value of a free press. Yes, we must be willing to put ourselves in a less-comfortable place in explaining what we do. Yes, we must rededicate ourselves to make sure all views are represented in our work. (Not that any of this is new.) But even at a time when truth is defined by personal beliefs and not by facts — what has been called a journalism of affirmation versus a journalism of verification — we cannot give in. We must stay true to our values. We must promote the honest truth — whatever that may be.

The self-loathing that has been a common thread among journalism pundits since President Trump's victory is not in the spirit of why we became journalists. President Obama was a master of promoting his ideas when he ran. So was President Trump. For those of us outside the media centers of power, the voter anger was readily apparent and found its way into our news columns.

And for the most part, the national press told the truth about Trump and Clinton. That so many voters chose to listen to the falsehoods about Clinton and to ignore the behavior of Trump is their right. And no one can seriously condemn the press for undercovering Clinton's email problems. In the end, we must look in the mirror and decide whether we told the truth.

That's why I'm a journalist: to provide the public the truth. If half the country isn't listening now, we must accept that fact. But our responsibility remains the same.

Truth.

Bio

Peter Bhatia, a multiple Pulitzer Prize-winning editor who has spearheaded meaningful journalism and digital advances at numerous news sites across the country, is editor and vice president of audience engagement at The Cincinnati Enquirer and Enquirer Media. He joined the Enquirer in August 2015.

Bhatia was director of the Reynolds National Center for Business Journalism at Arizona State's Cronkite School of Journalism. He joined the university in June 2014, as visiting professor in journalism ethics after a long and successful career at The Oregonian in Portland, where he was editor.

His resume includes helping lead newsrooms that won nine Pulitzer Prizes, including six in Portland. He is a six-time Pulitzer juror. He is the first journalist of South Asian descent to lead a major daily newspaper in the U.S., running The Oregonian from 2010 to 2014. He previously was the paper's managing editor and executive editor, teaming with then-editor Sandra Mims Rowe. Rowe and Bhatia were named editors of the year by Editor & Publisher magazine in 2008. He served as president of the American Society of Newspaper Editors in 2003–2004 and is a regular speaker on contemporary journalism issues.

Bhatia was executive editor of The Fresno Bee, managing editor of The Sacramento Bee, editor of the York (Pa.) Dispatch and Sunday News, managing editor of the Dallas Times Herald, deputy managing editor of the San Francisco Examiner and a reporter and editor at The Spokesman-Review in Spokane, Washington.

He also is a leader in journalism education, having served for seven years as president of the national organization that accredits college schools of journalism and mass communication from 2007 to 2014. He has led or served on 20 Accrediting Council on Education in Journalism and Mass Communications accrediting teams in the U.S., Middle East and New Zealand. He has just returned to the presidency of the accrediting agency, elected to a new term in May.

Peter and his wife, Liz Dahl, have two grown children who live in Portland and Philadelphia, and one grandchild.

Career timeline

2015–present, editor and vice president of The Cincinnati Enquirer.

2014–2015, visiting professor at the Walter Cronkite School of Journalism, Arizona State University.

1993–2014, executive editor, editor and managing editor at The Oregonian in Portland, which won six Pulitzer Prizes during this time.

1993, executive editor of The Fresno Bee.

1989–1993, managing editor of The Sacramento Bee, which won two Pulitzer Prizes during this time.

1988–1989, editor of the York Dispatch and Sunday News in Pennsylvania.

1987–1988, managing editor at the Dallas Times Herald.

1981–1987, news editor and deputy managing editor at the San Francisco Examiner, which won a Pulitzer Prize during this time.

1980–1981, page 1 editor at the Dallas Times Herald.

1977–1980, copy editor and assistant news editor at the San Francisco Examiner.

1975–1977, reporter/copy editor at The Spokesman-Review in Spokane, Washington.

SUSANA SCHULER

Executive vice president

Raycom Media

Source: Raycom Media

Imagine one day you are in a courtroom covering a trial with deep background information you've sourced ahead of time getting to know the victim's family, reviewing police reports, district attorney witness lists and previous rulings from the judge. The next week you are at the state capitol pressing the governor to implement a new law requiring access to hotel phones at all times by any age group for 911 emergency calls. Then that weekend you walk side-by-side with cancer survivors as part of a station-sponsored community fundraising event. Every day you have the chance to put your constitutional right to a free press to use. You question, dig, demand answers and open records access and explanations. You have the chance to use your powerful local broadcast reach to help one family or an entire community address a need by rallying the audience into action. Every day allows you to experience tremendous professional and personal rewards. That's why I am a journalist.

Unlike many of my peers, I wasn't born to be a journalist nor did I dream of this career growing up. As a first-generation American born to Chilean parents, freedom of the press and free voice in a democratic society were literally foreign to me. While I was raised in Texas, I spent my first years in Chile, then briefly in Germany as we worked our way to America fleeing the constraints of a potentially socialist regime with President Salvador Allende. Medicine was my family's background yet I wanted no part of it when I started at Texas Christian University. I dabbled in a variety of majors, never dreaming I would find my way to broadcast journalism. Luckily during my sophomore year, I overheard a conversation between a journalism professor and students, which intrigued me enough to take a class.

Pro tip

Today's aspiring journalist has an incredible opportunity via a station's digital assets to dip into a newsroom's current coverage and use that information in their cover email to show a news director how they would handle a particular story, newscast, social media post, tough call or sensitive interview as if they had been working in the newsroom that same day. In my opinion that is one of the most effective ways to show your skills and your ability to assimilate into their newsroom as you seek employment.

The lure of putting my liberal arts education to use covering diverse subjects daily enticed me. Starting out as a general assignment reporter, that variety sustained me as did the ability to build relationships that afforded me critical information long before others could uncover it. Along the way, as I moved into various positions in the newsroom and eventually management, the enormity of the impact we as local journalists can have on a community sunk in. That responsibility still motivates me daily. Few professions provide the same challenges and personal rewards of helping an individual or an entire state, of exposing a wrong that needs to be right, of sharing the good in a community, in an individual. We as local broadcasters are licensed to serve by the federal government.

Those of us who take that to heart and respect, embrace and employ our First Amendment rights to serve our communities are richly rewarded. Rewarded with coverage and connections that impact our communities for the better. Rewarded with an audience who turns to us on all platforms for life-saving information when it matters most during times of breaking news, extreme weather and natural disasters. Rewarded when we seek the truth by fact-checking, finding all voices in a story, presenting the facts, inviting the audience into the process via editorially transparency and letting them draw their conclusions. Rewarded when we meet our community face-to-face and see the good, see the need and see the willingness to help one another. Daily as a journalist you have a tremendous responsibility and ability to impact the community you serve, which in turn can richly impact your own life professionally and personally. That is why I am a journalist.

Bio

In July 2016 Susana Schuler was promoted to executive vice president, content & operations for Raycom Media. In that role, Schuler oversees news, marketing, digital content, programming and research for the company. Schuler joined Raycom Media in February 2006 to oversee its news operations. Prior to coming aboard, she was VP/corporate news director for Nexstar Broadcasting Group in Irving, Texas for nine years with oversight of that company's news operations across the country. Prior to joining Nexstar, Schuler served in news management roles in Pennsylvania, Indiana and Texas as well as anchor, reporter, producer and assignment manager roles in Texas and Pennsylvania.

Schuler is a cum laude graduate of Texas Christian University with a BS degree in broadcast journalism and a minor in business. She serves on the ABC board of governors as well as the Carole Kneeland Foundation and the Broadcast Advisory Board of the Associated Press. She currently serves as president of the Alabama Christian Academy President's Council. Schuler also volunteers for the American Cancer Society, Race for the Cure and the American Red Cross. Previously she served on advisory boards for the University of North Texas, Ball State University and Eastern Illinois University. In 2010, the Radio Television Digital News Foundation honored Schuler with the First Amendment Service Award for her work in championing First Amendment rights of journalists across the country. In 2002, Broadcasting & Cable Magazine named Schuler one of the Next Wave of Women in Communications to watch in the future. She is a first-generation American born to Chilean parents. As a newswoman, she has the dubious distinction of giving birth to her younger daughter on September 11, 2001. Schuler, her husband Ray Willingham and younger daughter Monica live in Montgomery, Alabama. Their older daughter, son-in-law and grandson are part of the U.S. Army, thanks to her son-in-law's enlistment in 2010.

Career timeline

2011, received Radio Television Digital News Foundation First Amendment Award.

2006–present, Raycom Media vice president, including executive vice president since 2016.

2002, recognized by Broadcasting & Cable Magazine as one of the Next Wave of Female Media Executives to Watch.

1997–2006, corporate news director at the Nexstar Broadcasting Group.

1986–1997, various news management and anchor, reporter and producer positions in Indiana, Pennsylvania and Texas.

1988, graduated cum laude from Texas Christian University.

JAY SHAYLOR

Executive producer of "The Situation Room with Wolf Blitzer"

CNN

I write for a living.

It is never Shakespeare and, when I am in a hurry, it is not terribly legible, even to me. But it has never been hard.

As a television reporter and producer, I have pounded out pieces and scribbled down scripts at a pace that leaves little time for reflection or self-doubt. I have dictated stories over a phone while standing in the wreckage left by an EF-5 tornado, composed copy while seasick on a boat in the Gulf of Mexico and written an introduction for an anchor to read on a dry-erase board while lying on my side under a camera. Now, as an executive producer, I am often called on to revise — or even rewrite — the toughest stories at the very last minute.

I like to think I have mastered the art of explaining who, what, when, where and how in ways equally concise and captivating.

But writing this — explaining *why* I am a journalist — was a task I found far more difficult. That's because the simplest answer for me is also the least fulfilling for you: I am a journalist because I always was one.

Still, there is a difference between knowing something and doing something with what you know.

Let me explain.

My route to becoming a professional journalist ended up being far more circuitous than I imagined it would be when I co-anchored my third-grade class video while daydreaming of replacing John Chancellor and Tom Brokaw. It was

no secret to my family that I would be a broadcaster. I talked about it — and everything else happening around me — incessantly.

In 10th grade I learned the basics of newswriting from Kay Horton, my journalism teacher, who marked up our stories as sharply as any professional editor and taught me many of the skills I still use today. "If it bleeds, it leads," she would say, reminding us of a slightly grotesque, but oft-quoted journalism axiom that you find the heart of the story — the blood — and start there. I went on to be co-editor of the school newspaper, attended journalism conferences and did an internship at the NBC affiliate in a town nearby. When a tornado knocked down a tree in my backyard, I covered it.

But after turning a few stories for one of the campus newspapers during my first weeks at the University of Virginia, I decided my heart was not in it. I wanted to try other things. I got involved in extra-curricular organizations and accepted leadership roles in student government. And while I took the few newswriting classes offered by the English department, I somehow lost my drive to break into journalism — although in the back of my mind I guess I was secretly convinced I somehow would.

By the beginning of my fourth year I settled on becoming a First Amendment lawyer, a dream that died a few months later when I contracted the flu, slept through three alarms and missed the LSAT.

After graduation I took a job with a consulting firm in Washington, D.C. It was about as far away from journalism as I could get. I hated it. Three years, three jobs and two cities later, I had moved from consulting to marketing to public relations, but I was still unfulfilled. My girlfriend at the time — now my wife — was starting her second year of medical school and was surrounded by people who loved what they did.

Then, one morning, I watched the terror attacks of 9/11 unfold as I was readying for work at a small dot-com company in Richmond, Virginia. I was in the car when the first tower fell. When I arrived at the office, I found the entire staff gathered around the only TV in the building — the one I insisted I needed on my desk to watch the news. I stayed with them for a few minutes. Then I left. I drove home and spent the next several hours glued to the television. As others were trying to understand what was unfolding in New York and Washington, I kept asking myself why I was not there explaining it.

The next day, I started looking at journalism programs.

One year later, as a student in the Graduate School of Journalism at Columbia University, I was there, explaining it. I covered the first anniversary of the attacks by walking the entire 19-mile length of Manhattan during a bagpipe and drum processional. I went down into "the pit," the scar left in the ground of Lower Manhattan where the towers once stood. I felt the raw emotions — the anger and pain mixed with optimism and resolve to rebuild. And I told the story of the men who walked into that hell and never looked back.

I have never looked back, either.

The terror attacks did not make me a journalist. Inside, I always was one. I knew it. I just didn't know what do to with it. From the time I was a little boy, I wanted to be where the story was. I wanted to know first. And I wanted to tell others. What that September day did do was solidify for me that being a journalist is not just a job, it is a calling. My professors at Columbia taught me it is a responsibility. And the people whose stories I have told have taught me it is a sacred trust.

Pro tip

Your job is to report the truth — accurately and completely. Every time. So even if your mother says she loves you, check it out. Not everything you are told or read — especially on the internet — is true. There is a lot of information that is intentionally falsified, accidentally distorted or incompletely reported. Once it gets published — especially online — it replicates exponentially, is picked up by other news outlets and eventually appears to be true. It is your job to confirm information. Get multiple sources. Check your facts. Then check them again. It is always better to be right than to be first. It is never OK to be wrong.

The framers of our democracy understood that. Journalism is the only profession protected by the Constitution. The enumerated right of a free press exists because our founders knew that in order for our country to work, journalists must be able to point out when it is not working. "The press was protected so that it could bare the secrets of government and inform the people," Supreme Court Associate Justice Hugo Black wrote in his concurring opinion in New York Times Company vs. United States. "Only a free and unrestrained press can effectively expose deception in government."

As a journalist I am not just allowed to speak truth to power, I am encouraged to do it. I have questioned candidates, members of Congress, presidents and a king. I have challenged the head of an energy company over his handling of an oil

leak, demanded answers from a bank CEO who was using deceptive practices to scam customers and pushed the chief lobbyist of the insurance industry over why one of his companies refused to cover a woman's brain surgery. I have covered trials, had a story used as evidence in federal court and seen a piece I produced screened during a congressional hearing. Journalism has opened doors for me I never thought I would see — much less enter — as a child growing up in a small town in South Carolina. I have met extraordinary people — in the United States and around the world — who triumph despite despair.

The hours are long, the vacations are sparse and the pay — to start — is even sparser. I have missed family dinners, friends' birthdays and a few anniversaries. I have stayed up all day and all night, stood in the middle of devastation and seen people at their very worst. And while we feel what we do is important, it can be depressing to see how many people disagree: a 2013 poll by the Pew Research Center shows as many Americans think journalists contribute "not very much" or "nothing at all" to society as those who think we contribute "a lot."

Still, I love it.

So, why am I a journalist?

I am a journalist because I cherish the opportunity — from the White House to a shooting victim's house — to witness events as they unfold.

I am a journalist because I embrace the chance to help write the first draft of history.

I am a journalist because I get to learn something new every day.

I am a journalist because I believe it is a moral imperative not just to know something, but to do something with what I know.

But above all, I am a journalist because I always was one and cannot imagine being anything else.

Bio

Jay Shaylor is the executive producer of "The Situation Room with Wolf Blitzer," CNN's flagship two-hour daily newscast covering breaking news, national security, international affairs and politics. Additionally, he helps produce CNN's award-winning election coverage and special events. Since taking the helm in October 2013, he and his team have been nominated for four News and Documentary Emmy Awards.

Previously, Shaylor served as the senior producer of ABC's "Good Morning America" overseeing editorial content and production of the broadcast during the evening and overnight hours. In 2012, Shaylor was part of the senior leadership team responsible for moving "Good Morning America" into first place in the competitive morning show ratings race — ending a 16-year winning streak by NBC's "Today Show." During his career at ABC

News, Shaylor also served as one of Diane Sawyer's anchor producers in the "GMA" studio and control room, produced investigative and spot news stories and was "GMA's" primary anchor and coordinating producer in the field during breaking news.

Shaylor is a Peabody, Murrow and Emmy Award-winning journalist. Before moving behind the camera as a producer, he was an on-air reporter for WSET-TV in Lynchburg and Roanoke, Virginia, where he won two Virginia Associated Press Awards.

Shaylor received a Master of Science with Honors from the Columbia University Graduate School of Journalism and was awarded a Pulitzer Traveling Fellowship — the school's highest honor. Before becoming a broadcast journalist, Shaylor spent four years leading the marketing and public relations operations of two dot-com companies. He holds a bachelor's degree in American history from the University of Virginia, where he was chosen for one of the university's most prestigious honors: living in one of the Thomas Jefferson-designed student rooms on The Lawn. He currently resides in Washington, D.C. with his wife and two children.

Career timeline

2013–present, executive producer of CNN's "The Situation Room with Wolf Blitzer."

2011–2013, senior producer at ABC's "Good Morning America."

2006–2010, producer and anchor producer at ABC's "Good Morning America."

2003–2005, reporter at WSET-TV, the ABC Affiliate in Lynchburg and Roanoke, Virginia.

2003, graduated from the Graduate School of Journalism at Columbia University.

1999–2002, worked as a consultant and marketing/public relations executive at three companies in Washington, D.C. and Richmond, Virginia.

Young journalists

People who enter journalism these days do so — or should, at least — with a clear understanding that the field is undergoing a major disruption, and is often under attack.

So what is so attractive about journalism? After all, journalism and mass communication degrees are popular with about 200,000 college majors nationwide, although the numbers have been declining slightly, according to a University of Georgia survey.

To end this book, I wanted to check in with some of my former students who have all graduated with journalism degrees from TCU in the past few years and went into journalism well-aware of the trials facing the industry — and the opportunities to make a difference.

The economic and audience challenges are clear, but there is also a personal challenge of entering a field when a lot well-intentioned of family and friends may give you a funny look when you say you want to be a journalist.

The need is great. As should be clear by now, journalism is indispensable to democracy, and for this democracy to keep working, we need dedicated young people to enter and invigorate journalism. It's certainly not a place for people who just want a paycheck or some form of celebrity. Now, more than ever, the best and brightest are needed.

For those who do decide journalism is the place for them, there are unparalleled opportunities for smart, eager and innovative people to help chart the evolving future for this very necessary work.

Work Cited

Becker, L., Vald, T. and Simpson, H.A. (2014). "2013 Annual Survey of Journalism Mass Communication Enrollments Enrollments Decline for Third Consecutive Year." Journalism & Mass Communication Educator, 69(4), 349–365.

ALEX APPLE

Reporter/anchor at WCAX-TV, Burlington, Vermont

Contributor, POLITICO and Professional Media Group

I had a vivid imagination as a child. My wonderful mother used to say she could always tell when I was not feeling well because she did not hear me running in our playroom that was just over her bedroom.

A lover of sports, I had a plastic basketball goal and two tackling dummies to play football and basketball to my heart's content in the playroom. I would make up games in my head until I was simply exhausted.

However, I knew at a young age that there was something I liked about writing and journalism too. When I was running up in the playroom I was also commentating on the games that I was making up in my head or playing with my dad. Often I would even write a game recap in a spiral notebook that I had. I guess those were my first gamers.

Fast-forward a decade and I am a senior at Texas Christian University about to graduate early with a degree in journalism and political science. Go to law school or go into journalism? That was my dilemma.

I had the good fortune during my time as a student of getting to write sports for Fox Sports and Yahoo as well as the Dallas Morning News. My sports-writing résumé had to be as good as any 22-year-old. My quandary was that journalists do not make much money out of college, and I knew that.

Undeterred by that fact, I leapt into the professional journalism world and moved to a part of the country that was totally unfamiliar to me. I moved to Vermont to report and anchor the news for WCAX, the CBS affiliate broadcasting in Vermont, part of New Hampshire and northern New York.

I learned more in my first six months working at WCAX than I had in four years in school (that's not a knock on TCU; it's wonderful, but no class or seminar replaces doing something on a daily basis).

Pro tip

Journalism is a lifestyle. You have to love the business, but there is reason to love it. The strength of American democracy depends on the quality of the public's information.

I also learned why I love journalism. There are few things in this world that we can improve upon every day … writing is one of those things. I played basketball a lot growing up. There will come a time when my body no longer allows me to play. I love golf, but my time will come in that sport as well. Yet, every day of my life I can become a better writer and storyteller, and quite frankly, I have always been in a race against myself to become the best writer I can be.

I also love the people one meets as a journalist. I spent many days in 2016 traveling the country covering the presidential election, and I saw so many communities, so many parts of America that I might not have seen otherwise. Of course, meeting people can be difficult as well. Some days as a journalist and broadcaster, you meet people on the best days of their life: a lotto winner, the

winner of a big election, a heroic firefighter. But on other days, you meet people on the worst day of their life. This is tough.

I will never forget the tragic crash caused by a wrong-way driver on the inter-state where five 16-year-olds were killed coming home from a concert. I will remember the crying mothers whose sons and daughters were killed by a stray bullet. Undoubtedly, the journalists that cover scenes such as 9/11 or the Sandy Hook tragedy will never forget those days either; how could you?

I have heard many older journalists say that the job will make you cynical. This has never been the case for me. Even in the midst of tragedy, I have learned things about the better side of human nature that give me hope.

As a journalist four years into my career, I feel the same about the profession as the eight-year-old boy who commentated his own imagination in his parents' house. There are few feelings for me richer than knowing you told a great story, a great feature or broke important news. That, for me, is the immense reward from the job.

The world of journalism is ever-changing. A decade from now, it will most certainly have morphed into something new again. For that reason, I have always tried to cultivate as many of my skills as possible. Well-rounded journalists are the ones that succeed nowadays. You must be able to do it all.

For that reason, I have continued writing even while working in television. I have freelanced for POLITICO, and I write sports magazines (in their entirety) for a company out of Florida. You never know what skill you will need for your next job. The answer is usually: all of them.

Some old traditions still linger in the business, but they will surely pass as today's 20-somethings and 30-somethings grow up to become the old hands in the newsroom. These changes do not scare me, and they shouldn't engender fear in you. Embrace the change. Embrace what makes you great.

Lastly, my faith in the profession is unwavering for a more altruistic reason. What some politicians and others do not realize when they criticize the media (yes, I acknowledge, the profession is not above reproach) is that the strength of American democracy depends on the strength of the public's information.

Without journalists, storytellers and dogged pursuit of truth, to whom are public servants accountable? What separates American democracy from other states is freedom of the press, freedom of speech. An informed public is vital to America's long-term health. The more time we take to understand one another, the better country we become.

I'll end with a quote from my idol in the profession, Scott Pelley of CBS News, speaking at the end of a January 2015 evening news broadcast:

> Most freedoms are limited. Gun ownership is restricted. You're free to travel but you're not free to run red lights. So why is freedom to publish, freedom to speak, absolute? Because there is no democracy without journalism … The enemy knows our vulnerability. Silence is the end of freedom.

Bio

Alex Apple was born in Nashville, Tennessee and graduated from Texas Christian University with a degree in journalism. He covered college athletics for Fox Sports and Yahoo, wrote for the Dallas Morning News and freelanced for POLITICO. He is an anchor and reporter for WCAX, a CBS affiliate in Burlington, Vermont, and he is a senior writer for Professional Media Group.

Career timeline

2014–2016, reporter/anchor at WCAX-TV in Burlington, Vermont.
2016, contributor at POLITICO.
2013–2016, senior writer for the Professional Media Group.
2013–2014, college sports reporter at the Dallas Morning News.

LEXY CRUZ

News producer

KDFW-TV, Dallas

There has always been this drive inside of me to help others.

You know how some people say running toward danger is just a part of their job? Well, there is no real running in my profession — unless you call my Olympic-worthy race-walk to the control room a "run." It's the meaning behind the phrase that keeps me coming back — having the ability to protect others.

I want to protect our ability to be the first draft of history. I want to protect the needs of those who depend on the government, law enforcement or other organizations. I want to protect the sanctity of downright facts. I want to protect people.

That's why I got into journalism — the idea of serving my community, being an unbiased middleman, exposing amazing tales of heroism or wicked crimes. My job lets me give the world just a little more balance. I have the chance to be part of something much bigger than myself by spreading truths and knowledge.

Days after graduating from Texas Christian University, I found my entire life packed into a 2001 Honda Accord heading to a city I had never laid eyes on. I have met very few journalists who have only worked in one town and, even less likely, one news station their entire career. The nomad life is typical in this line of work, but home is home. I knew the fastest way to get back home to the Dallas-Fort Worth area was to leave as soon as possible. Like the many journalists ahead of me, I had to put in my time at a smaller television market.

I worked and lived in Augusta, Ga. during my first two years out of college. There, I found other diehard journalists who wanted the exact same thing as I did — to hold people accountable and tell stories that made a difference.

The small market grind is something that grows both character and ability. You learn to multitask like you never thought imaginable when you're forced to handle the jobs of three or four people. It's definitely hard work, but the feeling of accomplishment afterward makes the tireless hours worth it.

An intense ice storm hit the Augusta area. My apartment along with nearly every other home in our coverage area was left without power. These are the moments that kick you out of comfy college mode. I didn't care that I wasn't going to sleep in my own bed for the next few days. I didn't mind driving on ice and pushing my car up a hill to get to work. I had a job to do. I was going to work to bring the news to people in dire need of it.

Coverage of that ice storm also drove home the fact that a journalist has to know where to find their audience. Our viewers hung onto our every post, every livestream, every newscast. Many of our viewers had no power, meaning no TV to watch our newscasts. We made sure our content online and on our app was just as good or better than the product that hit the airwaves.

There was no time to think about myself that week. I was focused on what our audience needed, what information certain counties were looking for, what my neighbors were asking about. I was lucky to have this experience and feel like my work really made an impact.

Pro tip

In journalism, every new day is a blank slate. The mistakes or achievements you made yesterday are in the past. Live in the present and press forward to be the best you've ever been.

In these first few years, you also see people come and go in the news business. I have found your first job in journalism can really make or break the longevity of your life in news. A strong news station that is willing to mold you and push you to try new things can set you on the path to succeed. A news station that over-works you and fills you with resentment will send you whistling toward a cushy public relations job in six months.

I was lucky enough to fall deeper into journalism. My obsession with social media and digital-first news helped rocket me from market 113 to 5. Yes, I have worked my way back home to Dallas! The ability to serve the community that helped shape the person I am today is indescribable. I can truly see our impact when I hear people mention certain moments in coverage or see stories shared between my aunts or high school friends.

Of course, there are days I drive home in a weeping mess — the news of the day hitting too close to home. I was out of town on July 7, 2016—when a gunman shot and killed five police officers while injuring nine others during a peaceful protest in Dallas. My mini-vacation was immediately cut short. Once at work, we worked hard and thoughtfully. We heard rumors of more attacks coming, sights of men on roofs put police and citizens on edge, misunderstandings near police headquarters put us on air in the middle of the day. The only thing that cut the panic in our minds was the kindness and forgiveness pouring out of the community's heart. Gifts and good thoughts created a safe place outside the Dallas Police Department headquarters.

I didn't become a journalist to live an easy, pain-free life. I know I can handle the stress and pressure by focusing on the positive. We have the ability to come into people's homes and bring them stories of love, loss and passion. That's why I became and will continue to be a journalist.

Bio

Lexy Cruz is a news producer at KDFW-Fox4 News in Dallas, Texas. She previously produced on-air and online content in Augusta, Georgia at WRDW. She is passionate about keeping ethical journalism alive and seizing media platforms ahead of its audience.

Career timeline

January 2015–present, news producer, KDFW-TV in Dallas.
2013–2015, news producer and digital content creator, WRDW-TV, Augusta, Georgia.
December 2015, graduated from Texas Christian University

ANDREA DRUSCH

Congressional reporter

National Journal

Source: Chet Susslin/National Journal

At the end of a semester-long internship in Washington, D.C., a veteran co-worker gave me a critical bit of career advice. I was thoroughly enjoying spending my final months of college in the nation's capital, but I was worried I hadn't learned enough about politics to accept a job there after graduation. I told her I was considering enrolling in a grad school program to learn more before returning.

"Just take the job," she told me. "A year working here will be the master's degree."

To this day that's how I like to think of my job, as a continuing education. Journalism is one of the few careers where learning on the job is not just acceptable, it's expected and critical. And whether I'm traveling to a new place with a campaign or meeting new people on the Hill, each day offers new experiences that shape me both personally and professionally.

Nowhere was that more true than covering campaigns for the 2014 and 2016 election cycles. Writing about Senate races meant starting from scratch every time news happened in a new state. I'd research candidates' political backgrounds and spend hours studying each state's political history. Then I'd call up the people who know the state best: former state party chairs, in-state political strategists and local business leaders. For the national context, I'd lean on strategists in D.C., who could explain why national groups might spend in one race over another.

Before I ever got out on the trail, I'd essentially been through a self-guided sociology course. Traveling with candidates allowed me to then put it all together, watching them interact with voters, and experiencing parts of the country I'd never traveled to. I got to talk to people whose lives are totally different than mine, and see how the issues being debated in Washington were impacting people at the local level.

On a trip to Ohio, I planned to write about whether a former Democratic governor from Appalachia could wage a political comeback in a poor part of the state that had voted for him in the past, but chosen only Republicans in recent years. After a campaign rally in his hometown, the candidate suggested we make an impromptu visit to his childhood home. He wanted me to see the modest conditions he grew up in, to show why he believed he connected with people in the area in a way his wealthy opponent couldn't. He lost the Senate race, but made his point.

Pro tip

Learn from the best. In college I discovered I could pick up interviewing tricks by listening to Diane Rehm on WAMU. You can absorb a lot just by sitting next to experienced journalists in the newsroom and hearing how they deal with sources on the phone.

In Pennsylvania, I followed a Republican senator to a public hearing on the state's opioid crisis. Despite national strategists' prediction that he would lose re-election in a state that had voted Democrat for the past six presidential elections, he focused his attention on local issues in Democratic strongholds. While both he and Donald Trump pulled off surprising victories in Pennsylvania, the senator won his race on an entirely different coalition, one that included more than 100,000 Hillary Clinton supporters.

Most journalists I know would concede they didn't know much about their beat before they started covering it. But it's not hard to see how those experiences quickly make journalists into the subject-matter experts.

And while the overall career path is demanding, I still often feel like I'm being paid to be a student, honing a set of skills I can take with me to any number of other jobs, in journalism or another field.

Bio

Andrea Drusch is a native Texan and 2011 graduate of the Schieffer School of Journalism at Texas Christian University. She studied in Washington, D.C. as part of the Schieffer School in Washington, then went on to work at

POLITICO for two and a half years as a web producer and reporter. She covered the 2014 and 2016 Senate races for National Journal's Hotline, before moving on to cover the Senate for National Journal.

Career timeline

2016–present, congressional reporter at National Journal.

2014–2016, senate race correspondent for the National Journal's Hotline, covered the 2014 midterms and 2016 Senate races.

2012–2014, web producer and reporter at POLITICO.

2011, graduated from the Schieffer School of Journalism at Texas Christian University.

LAUREN GALIPPO

Associate producer

"CBS This Morning"
CBS News

My dad taught me how to recite author Tom Hopkins' Champion Creed when I was eight years old. I learned a line at a time until I had it down. I was too young to understand the value in it but quickly realized he was instilling in me confidence to know that: "I am not judged by the number of times I fail, but by the number of times I succeed; and the number of times I succeed is in direct proportion to the number of times I can fail and keep on trying." He taught me that I was capable of anything and to never settle for second-best. We put together dream boards because, as dad reinforced, "What your mind conceives, your mind achieves." Eighteen years later, those lessons have led me to a place of resilience, happiness and success.

To say I was eager to set my career in motion is an understatement. I graduated from Texas Christian University on a Saturday in May of 2013, moved to New York City on Sunday, and started working at CBS News that same week. I remember talking to Bob Schieffer — the namesake of TCU's College of Communication and a mentor of mine — about my start date. I was confused why people kept asking me if I wanted to take a break post-graduation. As suspected, Mr. Schieffer told me, "Lauren if I were you, I'd fly there tomorrow!" And that is exactly what I did. Getting the job at the Tiffany Network a month before gradu-ation was no fluke. I put in the hours (and hours), worked with a sense of urgency, was persistent and continue to be to this day. There is no substitute for hard work.

The summer after my junior year at TCU, I took an internship at an independ-ent television station back in my home state of California, in sunny San Diego (sadly, no Ron Burgundy to be found there). It was my first dose of early morning television hours, and by early morning, I mean the middle of the night. If you are an adrenaline junkie, morning television is for you. I personally thrive off being the first one up and the energy that follows. Walking into the newsroom in the dark, you never know what each morning is going to bring. Plus, there is something so satisfying about getting loads of work done before some people even start their day (swiftly highlighting and checking off things on the to-do list is rewarding).

One morning, I was on assignment with a crew when a different cameraman called me and said he needed help with a story. A U.S. Navy ship was returning from deployment. He didn't have a reporter with him, and I hadn't done any on-air work outside of class, but I was willing to fly by the seat of my pants. When we got there, dozens of family members and friends had gathered to greet their loved ones. It was an emotional day and I had not thought about what I would say to put them at ease. Suddenly, the cameraman passed me the microphone and said, "Here, start talking to them." Being forward-thinking — but nervous — I asked the spouses, parents and children what they were most looking forward to and what was on the day's agenda. But I also asked them how they cope with their loved ones being overseas for long periods of time. It was pretty neat to then see each one of the interviewees lock hugs with the one we had been discussing. A game of connecting the dots. Pure joy. They ended up using my interviews, though just the cutaways. It was an incredible hands-on learning experience!

After my internship in San Diego was over, I headed to our nation's capital for the Schieffer School in Washington Program. The prestigious program included classes on top of a full-time internship at a news organization for a select group of junior and senior students. But only one student landed the internship at CBS News. That year, the student was me. When Mr. Schieffer's team called to ask what show I wanted to work for I thought, "I get to choose?" I was simply so grateful that I had been picked to work there. When faced with choosing between my mentor's show ("Face the Nation") and the network's morning show ("CBS This Morning"), I was completely torn. I grew up with Ann Curry on in my living room every morning; I always dreamed of working for a morning television show. However, how could I tell the news legend himself that I was going to pick the other man in the fight? Ultimately, I followed my heart and decided to work with the morning team. Today, Mr. Schieffer and I agree it was the perfect choice!

Going into the Washington Program, I knew I wanted to exceed expecta-tions — both my personal expectations and those in place at my internship. I decided beforehand that I was going to be the first one in and the last one out. I would be a "yes woman" in the best way. When a producer needed an extra person on a shoot, I was the first one to raise my hand; when they needed a presser to be logged, I was the first one to say I'd do it; and when it was time for a coffee run, I was already headed to Starbucks with a cardboard box for any drinks I couldn't fit in the two carriers (thinking outside — and inside — the box!). No job was too small.

When the senior producer asked the interns who would be willing to wake up even earlier to help out with an incoming anchor I immediately said, "Pick me!" See, at the time, my current boss (Norah O'Donnell) was doing the morning show from D.C. on Fridays. I had met O'Donnell at the Schieffer Symposium at TCU in 2012 and had no idea at the time that our first encounter would not be the last. Today, I am her associate producer at "CBS This Morning." I have been on her team since day one at CBS News. Have a can-do, "yes" attitude no matter if you are the intern or producer. Trust me, it doesn't go unnoticed.

Pro tip

Start early, go long, go beyond expectations, be resourceful, be resilient with no excuses and be a happy warrior.

It is also extremely important to be a self-starter. In the weeks leading up to the third 2012 presidential debate, I knew that I wanted to be involved somehow. I was not sure exactly how I was going to manage that as an intern, seeing as it was in Boca Raton, Florida, but I decided to make it happen. I made myself valuable to the staff, figured out a way to get there, and pitched the idea to my senior producer. Word to the wise: always be overly prepared when pitching. That's how I ended up in Boca Raton, watching President Barack Obama and Mitt Romney on stage. History unfolded right in front of me and I was hooked on that notion. All my efforts came with an added bonus, because that January, post-internship and back in Texas, I returned to D.C. to help the team cover the 2013 inauguration.

The Washington Program, unfortunately, had to come to an end, but before heading back down South, there was one thing left to do. I had decided early on in my internship with "CBS This Morning" that I wanted to be part of the team as a full-time employee. I decided to get on a train from D.C. to New York City to meet with staff at the broadcast center. I spent a few energizing hours with team members there before finally dragging my feet back to campus. I made sure to thank all of the people at my internship and folks who had made time for me in the city; I maintained communication throughout the last semester with those same people. You do not want to leave an internship and then pop up in someone's email inbox months down the road when you need a job. It is important that you stay in touch with people who mentored or helped you in some way during your internships and later in your job. Forming strong, healthy work relationships is essential. Be genuine.

I found it challenging to go back to school when I was craving what some college students deemed "the real world." My last semester included, but was not limited to: 16 credits left to fulfill, an office job at my apartment complex to help cover rent and an internship with the morning show at Dallas/Fort Worth CBS affiliate (I didn't want to get off my game.) When "CBS This Morning" called in April with a job offer, I ran out of class to answer. I screamed at the top of my lungs as I cradled the phone in the bathroom of Beasley Hall — which happens to be the department of religion. Oops! It was, to this day, the easiest question I've ever had to answer. Unfortunately for my professors, it also made me the least focused I had ever been (don't ask me what I got on my finals). My apartment was packed and boxes shipped to the city before I even walked across that stage to receive my diploma.

I set similar standards for my new job as I had with the internship: start early, go long, go beyond expectations, be resourceful, be resilient with no excuses, and be a happy warrior. You will develop (and want) thick skin in the media industry. Obstacles met with a positive attitude and a smile on your face will make you appreciate those challenges. Each one is a learning opportunity. Embrace them and pull yourself back up by the bootstraps if you get down. Nothing good ever comes easy, but if you are willing to put in the work, your opportunities are endless.

The first piece I produced aired on national television just six months into the job as broadcast associate at "CBS This Morning." I had read about the Vine app in Time magazine, specifically that large corporations were using the six-second videos to advertise to consumers. I had some experience pitching ideas as we had to practice that in journalism school. I knew I had to present the entire picture with details, confidence and diligence. I ended up writing out the pitch at least 20 times and then practiced verbally pitching it in the mirror. I was sick-to-my-stomach nervous. But practice makes perfect! My first big pitch. I decided I was going to see it through start to finish — from pitch to script, producing, finding the characters, shooting with a crew, putting it together with an editor and finalizing the (many) pieces of the puzzle. I did it! I am still so proud of that first piece. I cannot emphasize enough the feeling you get when you witness your work play out on television. Yes, it is pretty awesome to see your name spelled out under the producer credit. But for me, it is more so knowing that I can make an idea into a reality. I am always reminded, "What your mind conceives, your mind achieves." (Thanks, Dad.)

It is a surreal honor to be writing an essay that will be bound in the same book as essays by media professionals I truly admire. I am eternally thankful for the opportunities my job endows, including working with some of the best producers, crew, and on-air talent in the business at "CBS This Morning," "60 Minutes,"

and the "CBS Evening News." I get to meet and shake hands with world leaders like His Holiness the Dalai Lama and Malala Yousafzai, the youngest-ever Nobel Prize laureate, who survived a shot to the head from the Taliban. I was at the White House to cover Pope Francis' trip to D.C.; in Florida for a story on Prince Harry and veterans at the Invictus Games; spent two weeks at the Republican and Democratic National Conventions; traveled to Las Vegas and St. Louis for the 2016 presidential debates; was on set working till 3:30 a.m. on election night; and co-produced Paula Broadwell's first national television interview since news of her affair with David Petraeus broke in 2012.

I wake up each and every day excited and eager to get to work. In the news business, you never know what the day will bring. New stories, new opportunities, new faces and a chance to share original reporting. I am proud of all that I have accomplished in the four short years since graduating college. I don't like to pinpoint one moment that defines my career thus far, because I know there will be many more to come, but I do find a lot of pure joy in the stories that inspire people. That includes the "feel-good" stories I have produced — a Massachusetts single mom who ran seven marathons on seven continents in a week; cancer patient Gracie West whose wish was granted when she met Pope Francis; or the one-handed high school football star who spent the day with the New York Giants and got to meet his role model Odell Beckham Jr.

For me, this is less of a J-O-B and more of a lifestyle. Sure, it's a lot of hard work, but when you find something you love to do, you will never really work a day in your life!

Bio

Lauren Galippo is an associate producer at "CBS This Morning" in New York City. Galippo joined CBS News in May of 2013 just days after graduating from Texas Christian University in Fort Worth, Texas. She started at the network as a broadcast associate for Norah O'Donnell (co-host of "CBS This Morning") and still works on O'Donnell's team.

Galippo was part of the CBS network's 2016 presidential election coverage, traveling and working at the historic 2017 inauguration; election night; the St. Louis and Las Vegas debates; and the Democratic and Republican National Conventions.

Galippo began her career as a reporter for the TCU Daily Skiff and a sports producer for TCU 360. She interned at KUSI in San Diego, California and at CBS 11 in Dallas/Fort Worth. Galippo was also the alumni relations coordinator for TCU journalism before being accepted into the Schieffer School in Washington, D.C. where she interned for her current employer, "CBS This Morning."

She graduated from TCU with a major in broadcast journalism and a minor in writing. Galippo is a Kappa Alpha Theta alumna. She resides in midtown Manhattan while her immediate family still lives in her childhood home in Southern California (with their two family Weimaraners).

Career timeline

2015–present, associate producer at "CBS This Morning."
2013–2015, broadcast associate at "CBS This Morning."
2013, intern at KTVT-TV in Dallas-Fort Worth.
2012, intern in the CBS News Washington, D.C. Bureau for "CBS This Morning."
2012, intern at KUSI-TV in San Diego.

ANDREA MASENDA

Assistant editor

ESPN

There is no denying the effect that sports have on people. Sports bring communities together, help cities thrive, transform lives and make us all optimistic — and sometimes delusional — believers in something. Sports unite us and sports stories inspire us. I grew up a sports fan and loved all things ESPN. I admired the culture and the diversity and made it my goal to find a way to eventually be a part of it.

Although I held a writing internship right after college, for the most part, much of my young career has happened at ESPN. I came to Bristol, Connecticut on a seven-month contract to help with college football. However, I didn't have any intention of going back to Texas when I was done (it's a really long drive) and this was my shot to make my dream a reality.

I wanted to earn a full-time job at ESPN — and I didn't have a Plan B. I just knew that I had to make every day count from the minute I walked in on my first day. I started as a production assistant in August 2014, and for the following seven months spent a bulk of my time cutting highlights, screening our programming and pitching story ideas to anyone who would read my emails.

After that, I got another contract position with ESPN Films, this time for eight months. Half of the time I worked as the production assistant for ESPN's annual ESPY Awards show. You know the one, it's powerful and funny and guaranteed to make you cry at least twice. It required a lot of organization, communication and reliability on my part, but I learned so much. I built a lot of great relationships in that role and was proud of the work we did on that year's show. When it was over,

I helped with ESPN's 30 for 30 series, another chance to learn from incredibly talented people and diversify myself within the sports realm of television.

I made the most of my free time in those positions. Every chance I got I was reaching out to people at the company that I admired to schedule time to meet with them and learn from them. I would come in early or stay late to shadow producers and study how they pieced together stories, or attempt to produce my own examples to show them what I could do. Rarely was there a workshop or speaker series that I didn't attend. I was just laser-focused on making myself the best candidate I could be, and in December of 2015, it finally paid off when the social media team hired me full-time.

I had fallen in love with social media as a journalism tool while at TCU, and having the opportunity to use the platform professionally had always been a goal of mine. Joining the team gave me a chance to produce creative video content for ESPN's official Snapchat Discover and Instagram accounts and even have a bit of my writing showcased on ESPN.com.

Pro tip

Take advantage of your opportunities and embrace challenges to get where you want to go.

Working in new media forces you to think differently, and luckily for me, let me showcase my creative side. I analyze the news and sports in different ways since I started this job. I'm constantly thinking of the most effective ways to interpret and execute stories on digital platforms.

Today, I feel incredibly indebted to the people who took a chance on me. Throughout my journey, there were certainly times where I wondered if I had the skills to excel in sports media — but finding a team that values my work and perspective meant everything to me. As I've gotten more comfortable, I've become incredibly confident as a producer, as a writer, and as an employee. In the spring of 2015, our Snapchat team was even nominated for a Sports Emmy Award for Best Digital Innovation. It was huge for all of us to see our hard work pay off, and I also think it was a strong indication of how valuable social platforms have become to news consumers.

I've grown a lot and am incredibly appreciative to work with the some of the most talented individuals in sports every day.

Honestly, we're all tested in our lives. You might be going through college right now, staying up all night and trying to find a way to get an A in Chimbel's class (good luck with that!). You might even think that this is as hard as it's going to get. Unfortunately, dear reader, I'm here to tell you that it gets a lot harder. And I mean that in the best, most encouraging way possible!

Here's the thing — school is hard, but getting a job you love is even harder. Once you finally do get that job, hanging on to it and excelling in it is equally hard, maybe harder.

You will never in your life stop fighting and working hard for the things you want and the things that make life meaningful, so embrace it.

Embrace challenges, the late nights and research. Embrace the work that forces you get organized, that overwhelms you at first, that feels impossible when it's first assigned. Those are the things that make you proud upon completion. There's nothing better than being proud of what you've done and how hard you worked.

Moving on — let's talk about ideas. I used to hate coming up with story ideas when I was in college. Coming to class with three specific story ideas always felt forced to me and I hated doing it. So before we go any further, I want to take this time to thank Aaron Chimbel — an honest man and a damn good professor — for always asking for story ideas.

Today my life revolves around them. Finding good ones is mandatory, but finding great ones sets you apart. No matter where you work, media is a competitive industry, and finding a great story is what keeps the machine running better than the rest. Moral of the story — ideas are forever. Learn to love them, hunt for them and when one gets the green light, knock it out of the park.

My next advice is to listen to people smarter than you. Every single day of your life in this field you are going to come across someone who knows more, who's seen more, and sometimes you don't realize it because you're too busy talking. Seek out people who are smarter than you and pick their brains. Ask to hear about their journey. Some people might not have time for you, but some will. The ones that do can change your life. Be a good listener. Be curious. Soak in what they tell you and find a way to apply it your work. (Oh, and trust me, people love to give advice too, it makes them feel like they've really got their lives together!) Writing this feels great, by the way.

Lastly, understand that there will be rejection. People are going to tell you no. People are going to think that you aren't the right fit, or that you need more experience. Getting rejected is a fundamental part of getting where you are going. I've been turned away quite a few times in life, I just never internalized it. I believed in myself and that my time was going to come. I just had to keep working, I had to keep learning, I had to keep moving in order to become the person that was going to get the yes.

I know that I'm going to hear no again, probably more times than not, but I'll never stop chasing down the yes.

Bio

Andrea Masenda graduated from TCU in December 2013. She currently works as an assistant editor in the social media and digital content group at ESPN after serving in various production assistant roles.

Career timeline

2016–present, assistant editor at ESPN.
2015–2015, production assistant, the ESPYs.
2014–2015, production assistant at ESPN.
2014–2014, promotions assistant at Cumulus Media.
December 2013, graduated with a bachelor's degree from TCU.

RYAN OSBORNE

Staff reporter

Fort Worth Star-Telegram

The question surprises me, but I guess it shouldn't.

"Isn't journalism dying?"

This is the response I sometimes get when I tell people about my job as a newspaper reporter. They wonder why, as a 24-year-old, I wanted to enter such a shaky business.

I can't blame them. The warning signs were all around.

Readers have been rapidly shifting from print to digital for years, and newspaper companies have been trying to catch up. Not only are papers having to put more emphasis on digital, they are still having to maintain revenue, which for many newspapers is still rooted in the print product.

Layoffs have become common news across the country, and jobs, especially for young graduates with little experience, aren't easy to land.

There are other concerns that probably would make an aspiring journalist weary.

Most journalists enter the industry because of a deep passion for telling stories and providing impactful information to the public. But completing that important work requires time and resources. With smaller staffs, the opportunity for long-term projects might not always be available.

But here's where I believe younger journalists have an advantage, and why I find value in my work.

We can understand the challenge of reaching a different audience — a digital audience — because we are that audience.

We grew up with the internet. As social media evolved, we learned it on the go, because it was the way we communicated with our friends. As a journalist, I try to use that nativeness to technology to my advantage.

What are my friends talking about on Facebook? What's trending on Twitter? What's important to people in my social media circles? Can I package that into a story?

Take, for instance, my daily routine at work.

The first thing I do is check Twitter. Then I check CrowdTangle, an application that compiles trending stories on Facebook. Then I check email, and then Twitter again, and then CrowdTangle. I'll also glance periodically at Chartbeat, which shows how many people are currently reading your story, how they reached your story, and the average time they are spending on your story.

Pro tip

Go to your audience. Readers can choose what they want to read, when they want to read it, and how they want to read it. They don't rely on a daily newspaper to outline the stories of the day. Through social media, you have to bring your stories to them and know which ones they will care about.

For all the challenges technology has posed for newspapers, it has also given us this: A chance to know our audience like never before. Journalism is about telling stories that are important to your community — technology allows us to find those stories.

But while I feel comfortable using digital tools, I don't forget how quickly this business can change.

As I said, I'm 24. I can remember being a teenager and still reading my local newspaper in Oklahoma every day. It's how I got my news. Each morning, I'd fetch the paper from the yellow box at the end of our driveway, and unfold it on the living room floor, poring over box scores and game stories on my hands and knees. Eventually, I decided to make a career of it.

I started working for my high school newspaper. I absorbed columns by Rick Reilly and Bill Simmons and any other sportswriter I could find. I applied to a school with a good journalism school. I spent a week at a high school journalism camp. Nerdy, I know.

When I arrived at TCU in the fall of 2010, I thought I was ready. Now, seven years later, it's hard to believe I wasn't yet on Twitter. Snapchat and Instagram didn't exist. I didn't have a cell phone that could take video (RIP Blackberry).

But I never felt like the technology was something I had to practice to learn. In a way, it came naturally.

I used Twitter to keep up with my favorite teams. I followed the team accounts and the writers who covered them. I followed the players. I followed my friends, and we'd get into stupid arguments about those teams and those players.

I viewed Twitter as a hobby, not a crucial element of my career.

Meanwhile, in journalism school, I began to realize I enjoyed telling stories, whether they were those of athletes or not.

I covered the TCU athletics but also did an in-depth feature on how the administration was trying to improve campus diversity. I covered the TCU football team but also wrote about the aftermath of a fertilizer plant explosion in rural Texas.

When I graduated from TCU in 2014, I was working for the Star-Telegram as a part-time high school sports reporter. About a year later, I switched to a full-time position covering news.

As our newspaper continued pushing more digital content, we became more aware of which stories were popular with our readers. Some stories do well on Facebook, others do better on Twitter. Some, as we can see through Chartbeat, are highly searchable and discovered through keywords on Google.

The analytics — from Facebook shares and likes to Twitter engagements to pageviews — can seem overwhelming, but I try to embrace the numbers. Our job is to cultivate an audience and impact readers. The technology, something younger journalists are comfortable with, allows us to do that.

I don't view that as a reason to shift my focus from why I think journalism is important. Reporting, context and clarity have always been tenets of journalism, and they always will be. It's why I enjoy being a journalist, being able to tell a story that matters.

But I also enjoy being able to maximize who sees my work, and I can control that, to an extent, by navigating social media and understanding digital readers.

Here's an example of that. Recently, there was a rodeo scandal in the Fort Worth area that resulted in a lawsuit.

I did the initial story, mostly writing it from the information in the lawsuit, which alleged that three calf ropers lost a competition on purpose to guarantee a cut of a larger prize. The details were vague, but it was an interesting case. After I posted it on Facebook, it began to steadily gather readers.

Then, out of nowhere, the traffic on the story skyrocketed. As it turned out, a rodeo magazine shared the article on its Facebook page, driving most of the pageviews. It ended up as my most-read story of the year.

More than that, it showed me that an audience — albeit a niche one — was passionate about something I wrote. So I stayed on the story, following the lawsuit through court until I found a juicy document filed in the case.

I wrote a follow-up story and emailed it to the rodeo magazine that shared the first one. The story gained similar traction.

Were the pageviews why I was happy with the story? No. But I was able to recognize an audience, report a story for that audience and have the story make an impact among the audience's readers. Even for a goofy rodeo scandal, that was rewarding.

Bio

Ryan Osborne is a crime and breaking news reporter for the Star-Telegram newspaper in Fort Worth, Texas. He reports, writes and posts several stories online each day, along with pushing those stories on social media. Before that, he covered high school sports for the Star-Telegram. He also interned at The Dallas Morning News, and in college, ran a TCU football coverage website for Rivals.com.

Career timeline

2015–present, Star-Telegram crime and breaking news reporter.
2013–2015, Star-Telegram high school sports reporter.
2013, Dallas Morning News business desk intern.

DANIEL SALAZAR

County government reporter on the Wichita Eagle

Wichita, Kansas

One of my favorite pieces of writing is an essay by French existentialist Albert Camus called "The Myth of Sisyphus." Camus argues humanity's fate is similar to that of Sisyphus, the figure in Greek mythology that is punished by the gods to push a giant boulder up a hill for all eternity. Every time he pushes the boulder near the top, it rolls back down and he must start all over again. Camus argues our efforts to find meaning in a sometimes meaningless and chaotic world often end in failure. But Camus doesn't think that's reason for despair. We can find meaning in the struggle. We can invest ourselves in moving forward, onward and upward. Our efforts may not have universal meaning. But they can provide meaning to ourselves. Yes, it's difficult. Yes, it's frustrating when we are beset on all sides by obstacles. But continuing to fight and move forward, in resistance to apathy and nihilism, is worth it.

Most journalism students get that this is not an easy profession. The hours. The pay. The public's perception of the media. The shape of the industry. Even Journalism 101 rules are not necessarily easy. One of my professors had three rules for journalism: Don't assume, no clichés and get it right. Well, it's easy to assume. It's easy to use clichés. And it's very easy, as some media outlets show us, to get something wrong. Journalism looks difficult. It looks like climbing a steep hill. But then you start pushing the boulder.

You get your first story. You get your first compliment for your work. You get your first major byline. You get your first front page story. You start to gain confidence. But then you get your first nasty comment. You find out that, for some stories, literally nobody is going to call you back. You find out that sometimes public information officers aren't going to provide you with very good, accurate information. You find out, ironically, some spokespeople aren't good at speaking or giving you good quotes for a story. You hit roadblock after roadblock. The boulder will roll back down the hill many times in this profession. It can happen within stories multiple times. For instance, you may learn new details in the course of your reporting that mean you're going to have to rewrite the whole thing. On a larger scale, every story you finish means there's another one to be done. In a sense, even when you succeed and craft an important and impactful story, the boulder rolls back down to settle at the bottom of the hill. You must begin your next enterprise. But that's nothing to despair over. It's another opportunity to tell a great story or hold the powers at be accountable. Just remember: at the end of "Spotlight," the reporters came back to work the next day. Because a new boulder needed pushing.

Pro tip

It's about persistence. If what government officials and public relations people are saying doesn't make sense, press them on it. Your readers get better content when you're annoying and persistent and don't let roadblocks to information get in your way.

I cover local government at my current job. That's always the type of journalism that's interested me. I was a debate nerd in high school, so I was interested in politics and policy long before I ever took a journalism class. My goal is to provide a fair, open public forum for ideas. In the arena of politics, that's not an easy task, even to other journalists. One of my colleagues in Wichita is a crime reporter I highly respect. He's a guy who's extremely thorough. He double and triple checks the facts when he covers very sensitive crimes and cases. He's been working in newspapers for several decades.

After I covered a particularly long government meeting where the egos and partisanship were on full display, he approached me and gave me a compliment to my work. "I could never do what you do," he told me, the youngest reporter in the room. It was shocking praise that I thought I did not deserve. If anything, I could never do what he does: talking to families after losing their loved ones. But the point is that neither role is easy. There are roadblocks, both material and mental, in the way of doing our jobs. What matters is how we respond. What matters is that we use our knowledge and our compassion to greater ends.

The last lines of Camus' "The Myth of Sisyphus" are "The struggle itself toward the heights is enough to fill a man's heart. One must imagine Sisyphus happy."

After about a year and a half as a professional, that's how I view journalism. I'd be lying to you if I said it was always easy or always fun. It is a struggle. But it is toward the heights. It's in pursuit of lofty goals of a more informed, just society. It is a noble fight. Without the journalist, there are stories untold. Without the reporter at the local government meeting, there is a less informed public and, in all likelihood, more corruption and abuse of power. Don't let anyone tell you otherwise: Journalism is still a worthy profession. And more importantly, maybe it'll make you happy while you're working in it.

P.S. Don't take my word for it, Camus was a journalist too.

Bio

Daniel Salazar is a local government reporter for the Wichita Eagle newspaper in Wichita, Kansas. He covers Sedgwick County, which is the county that includes Wichita and its surrounding towns and cities. He attended Texas Christian University where he majored in journalism and political science with a history minor. He grew up in a military family all over the U.S.

Career timeline

2015–present, county government report at the Wichita Eagle in Wichita, Kansas.

May 2015, graduated from TCU with degrees in journalism and political science.

2014, intern in McClatchy's Washington bureau.

2014, business news intern at The Dallas Morning News.

Afterword: My life in journalism

BOB SCHIEFFER

CBS News legend

Source: CBS News

I'll say it upfront: journalism is not for everyone. For one thing, you have to work a lot on Christmas, at least in the beginning, and sometimes the pay is not much. But if you get good at it, the pay part will take care of itself and you may even get a Christmas or two off.

But here's the important part: if you're a little nosey, if you like to know things before other people do, if you like to see things with your own eyes, if you like to go places other people can't and talk to people who make the decisions that impact on all our lives (and ask them why they did what they did) and most of all have a little fun and maybe even make a difference even at an early age, then journalism is for you.

As I look back on more than half a century in journalism (yep, I am that old!), I got to do all that and more. I wanted to be a reporter from the time I saw my name for the first time in boldface type set atop a story I wrote for my junior high school newspaper.

I got my first job in journalism at a little radio station in Fort Worth the summer of my sophomore year at TCU and I've had a paid job in journalism ever since including the three years I spent in the Air Force when I was the editor of a base newspaper and several military publications.

It was during that first job that I learned the power that comes with a reporting job. The news director told me one day to call the mayor and get a comment on something that had happened at City Hall.

I was terrified and said, "He won't talk to me. He doesn't even know who I am."

"He knows where you work," the boss said. So I called the number, his wife answered and when I identified myself, she said, "Tom, it's Bob Shafer" (close enough for government work) and low and behold the familiar voice of Mayor Tom McCann came on the phone and he said, "What can I do for you Bob?"

I have to admit I'm still sometime amazed at the folks who take my calls, but a lot of them do (and a few don't).

Every job I had during those years as I went from the Fort Worth Star-Telegram night police beat to the local NBC affiliate Channel Five and on to CBS News in Washington seemed to me the best job a person could have.

Journalism to me was a great adventure — whether it was covering the cops in Fort Worth or the awful events like the assassination of John Kennedy and 9/11 or tracking down young Texans who were fighting the Vietnam War, or having the honor of being chosen to moderate three presidential debates.

"Journalism is the first draft of history," as the cliché goes, but the view from the front seat that journalism provides is unparalleled and the experiences beyond anything I might have imagined. As was the case in the hours after the death of President Kennedy when I answered that phone at the Star-Telegram and the caller turned out to be Lee Harvey Oswald's mother and another reporter and I drove her to Dallas.

Nor would I ever have imagined in those early years that one day I would moderate three presidential debates. During the 2008 debate I found myself sitting at a table between Barack Obama and John McCain. The millions upon millions of Americans who watched that debate heard and saw them, but I was close enough to see McCain taking copious notes as Obama spoke. And I was close enough to see that Obama took no notes, but from time to time simply drew a straight line across his note pad. What was that about? Was it some sort of Zen exercise? Was he pushing down as hard as he could with that pen to relieve tension? I still don't know but after he leaves the presidency, if I have the opportunity, it's the first question I'll ask him.

Some of my favorite moments came at small rather than large events or years after events had passed.

When I was writing my professional memoir, "This Just In," I interviewed many of those who had been a part of the stories I covered. I spent the good part of a day in 2004 with George McGovern who lost his run for the presidency in 1972 in a historic landslide.

"Did you ever get over it?" I asked.

"No, I never did," he told me, "and no one really ever does."

That helped me to understand just how much courage it takes even to compete in electoral politics at that level.

Once during an otherwise inconsequential White House press briefing during Gerald Ford's administration then-Secretary of State Henry Kissinger was brought in to give us the latest on some long-forgotten event. The press secretary stressed that Kissinger had only 20 minutes, not a second more.

Kissinger, ever the ham, said that as a college professor he was used to giving 40-minute lectures, he wasn't sure he could do it in 20 minutes, to which legendary reporter Helen Thomas retorted: "Then start at the end."

Even the Old Professor got a kick out of that one.

I said at the top that journalism was not for everyone but I loved every minute of it and moments like that one that made it so.

There are many ways to have a good life but I can't think of anything I could have done that would have been more satisfying — and for me anyway, more fun.

Bio

Bob Schieffer was CBS News' chief Washington correspondent and moderator of "Face the Nation" until his retirement in 2015. He returned to CBS in 2016 as a contributor to its coverage of the 2016 election. He has interviewed every president since Richard Nixon and moderated presidential debates in 2004, 2008 and 2012.

Schieffer is one of the few journalists to have covered all four major beats in the nation's capital — the White House, the Pentagon, the State Department and Capitol Hill. He served as interim anchor of "The CBS Evening News" from March 2005 until August 2006.

Schieffer is a member of the Broadcasting/Cable Hall of Fame and has won many other broadcast journalism awards, including eight Emmy Awards, one of which was for Lifetime Achievement, and two Sigma Delta Chi Awards.

Before joining CBS News in 1969, he was a reporter at the Fort Worth Star-Telegram and a news anchor at WBAP-TV (now KXAS-TV) in Dallas/Fort Worth.

He is the author of four books, including the 2003 New York Times best-seller, "This Just In: What I Couldn't Tell You On TV."

Schieffer and his wife, Pat, are both graduates of Texas Christian University, where the College of Communication is named in his honor.

INDEX

Check out these other titles to help advance your career in broadcasting! Find these and more at Routledge.com.

The Art of Editing in the Age of Convergence, 11th Edition **by Brian S. Brooks and James, L. Pinson**

The Art of Editing in the Age of Convergence remains the most comprehensive and widely used text on editing in journalism. This latest edition continues to shift the focus toward online multimedia as more and more people get their news that way. Amidst these changes, the authors continue to stress the importance of taking the best techniques learned in print and broadcast editing and applying them to online journalism. The reality is that most people now often first learn of breaking news on Facebook or Twitter and therefore, the challenge for journalists in this new media world is distinguishing the quality and dependability of their work from all the fake news and propaganda memes, now so common online. This book is designed to help serious news providers produce a product that is well-edited and grounded in the best practices of journalism.

Broadcast News Writing, Reporting, and Producing, 7th Edition **by Frank Barnas**

Broadcast News Writing, Reporting, and Producing, 7th Edition is the leading book covering all aspects of writing and reporting the news. It identifies the key concepts and terms readers need to know in the news gathering and dissemination process, and provides practical, real-world advice for operating in the modern day newsroom. New to the 7th Edition are profiles of working journalists who give readers a glimpse into the working life of modern reporters, producers, and directors. This new edition also covers important aspects of the use of social media. A new chapter on Portfolio Development will assist readers in developing the skills to advance in their careers. The text has also been updated to reflect new industry standards in modes of information gathering and delivery, writing style, and technology.

Think/Point/Shoot: Media Ethics, Technology and Global Change **Edited by Annette Danto, Mobina Hashmi, Lonnie Isabel**

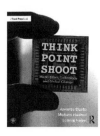

Think/Point/Shoot gives students a thorough overview of the role of ethics in modern media creation. Case studies emphasize the critical issues in global media ethics today in all stages of media creation from preproduction research and development, to production and post production. This volume features practicing filmmakers, journalists, and media creators who provide insight into dealing with real-world ethical dilemmas.